Talent Abroad

A Review of Ghanaian Emigrants

O)) OECD

This work is published under the responsibility of the Secretary-General of the OECD. The opinions expressed and arguments employed herein do not necessarily reflect the official views of the Member countries of the OECD.

This document, as well as any data and map included herein, are without prejudice to the status of or sovereignty over any territory, to the delimitation of international frontiers and boundaries and to the name of any territory, city or area.

Please cite this publication as:
OECD (2022), *A Review of Ghanaian Emigrants*, Talent Abroad, OECD Publishing, Paris, https://doi.org/10.1787/5342a9d4-en.

ISBN 978-92-64-69944-1 (print)
ISBN 978-92-64-72482-2 (pdf)
ISBN 978-92-64-85923-4 (HTML)
ISBN 978-92-64-38286-2 (epub)

Talent Abroad
ISSN 2790-282X (print)
ISSN 2790-2838 (online)

Foreword

Emigrants are often considered a loss for their country of origin but they can also play an important role in fostering trade and economic development, notably through the skills and contacts they have acquired abroad. If they choose to return, their re-integration into the labour market and society will be facilitated by the fact that they speak the local language, have specific social capital and possess local qualifications that are readily recognised by employers.

Drawing on the human resources of emigrants, however, necessitates maintaining links with them and pursuing policies adapted to the specific needs of each expatriate community. This entails, as a prerequisite, being able to identify precisely where, when and why people have left and what their socio-demographic characteristics and skills are, as well as gaining a proper understanding of the dynamics of the phenomenon and the aspirations of emigrants.

Statistical systems in countries of origin are generally poorly equipped to undertake this monitoring exercise. It is therefore helpful, if not essential, to compile information directly from destination country data sources. This is particularly challenging because it requires collecting data, based on comparable definitions and concepts, from a large number of countries across which emigrants are scattered. The OECD Database on Immigrants in OECD Countries (DIOC), which pools census and survey data, makes it possible to identify individuals over time by place of birth as well as by education and labour market status. It is a powerful tool for use in undertaking this mapping exercise, especially when complemented by available national sources (e.g. consular data, specific surveys, analyses of social networks) and many other international data sources.

This series of country reviews entitled "Talent abroad" aims to provide an accurate, updated and dynamic picture of diasporas by individual countries of origin. On this basis, and by building on cumulated experiences regarding the movements of diasporas, it is possible to formulate public policy recommendations on how best to engage with emigrants and mobilise their skills to support economic development in their country of origin.

This volume focuses on Ghana, which, in recent years, has experienced significant economic, social and political changes. In view of the scale of emigration by the Ghanaian population in the 21st century, the Ghanaian authorities are seeking to gain a better understanding of this pool of talent based abroad. To that end, this review was commissioned by the German Co-operation Agency (*Deutsche Gesellschaft für Internationale Zusammenarbeit*, GIZ). The GIZ's Programme Migration & Diaspora (PMD) supports partner countries in leveraging the positive effects of regular migration and diaspora engagement for their sustainable development. The PMD is implemented by the GIZ on behalf of the German Federal Ministry for Economic Co-operation and Development (BMZ). It is active in 23 partner countries around the world. The PMD supports partner countries in shaping development-oriented and socially responsible labour migration. It advises partner governments on migration policies and on promoting diaspora engagement for sustainable development.

The in-depth analysis of the Ghanaian diaspora presented in this OECD publication helps determine the economic potential of emigrants. How many emigrants are there, and where are they based? Are they of working age, and what is their level of education? What are the recent trends in terms of their number and socio-economic profile? What is their labour market presence in the host country and which occupations do they hold?

Acknowledgements

This report was written by Thomas Calvo, Taehoon Lee, Sara Mouhoud, Gilles Spielvogel and Marcela Valdivia Correa. The OECD Secretariat would like to thank the Deutsche Gesellschaft für Internationale Zusammenarbeit (GIZ) for their support in funding this study on behalf of the German Federal Ministry for Economic Co-operation and Development (BMZ). The Secretariat also thanks the participants of the Multi Stakeholder Dialogue, organised by GIZ, for their valuable feedbacks. Thanks are also due to Dominika Andrzejczak and Charlotte Baer for their assistance, to Jean-Christophe Dumont, Head of the OECD's International Migration Division, and to the members of the Division for their comments.

Table of contents

FIGURES

Follow OECD Publications on:

http://twitter.com/OECD_Pubs

http://www.facebook.com/OECDPublications

http://www.linkedin.com/groups/OECD-Publications-4645871

http://www.youtube.com/oecdilibrary

http://www.oecd.org/oecddirect/

Executive summary

Ghana is the second ECOWAS country with the largest migration flows to OECD countries

Migration flows from Ghana to OECD countries are the second highest among the countries of the Economic Community of West African States (ECOWAS), after Nigeria. Although growth in flows from Ghana to OECD countries has been slower than that from other ECOWAS countries, annual legal migration flows from Ghana more than doubled between 2000 and 2019, from 12 900 in 2000 to 23 000 in 2008 and to 27 400 in 2019.

The United States attracts the largest flows of Ghanaian nationals in the OECD area

Among OECD countries, the United States attracts the largest annual flows of Ghanaians, with more than 8 400 Ghanaian migrating to the country in 2019, followed by the United Kingdom, Italy and Spain. Between 2000 and 2019, these four countries received 85% of Ghanaian annual flows to OECD countries. Flows to Italy and Germany significantly increased over the past decade, reflecting a recent trend of diversification in destination countries.

The majority of residence permits issued to Ghanaian nationals by OECD countries are issued for family reasons

Since 2010, more than half of residence permits issued annually to Ghanaian nationals by European countries have been issued for family reasons, while roughly one-third have been issued for humanitarian reasons. Similarly, more than 70% of permanent residence permits issued by the United States are issued for family reasons, although temporary residence permits issued are mainly issued for educational purposes. In Europe, the United Kingdom is also the only country to grant a substantial number of permits for educational reasons to Ghanaian nationals.

Intentions to emigrate in Ghana are high, especially among young and unemployed Ghanaians

Between 2009 and 2018, 44% of Ghanaians expressed the intention to emigrate, a higher share than the average population living in ECOWAS countries (36%). However, these emigration intentions rarely materialise in the short or medium term, as only 17% of Ghanaians intending to emigrate consider doing so within a year, a lower share than in other West African countries. Emigration intentions in Ghana are substantially higher among young and unemployed individuals and the difficult employment situation is the main driver of emigration intentions in Ghana.

Nearly half a million Ghanaian emigrants live in OECD countries

The Ghanaian diaspora is almost equally distributed between African and OECD countries. In Africa, Ghanaian emigrants are primarily concentrated in the ECOWAS area and Nigeria alone hosts a fourth of the total diaspora. Five countries – the United States, the United Kingdom, Italy, Germany and Canada – account for almost 90% of Ghanaian emigrants living in the OECD area. Between 2000 and 2020, the number of emigrants from Ghana living in OECD countries registered a threefold increase. Although the United States and the United Kingdom hosted populations of Ghanaian emigrants of similar size in 2000, by 2020 the United States had become the leading destination in the OECD area. Ghana's total population represents 8% of the ECOWAS population, but Ghanaian emigrants account for 16% of all ECOWAS migrants living in OECD countries, reflecting a comparatively long history of extra-continental emigration and high economic growth.

The Ghanaian diaspora in OECD countries is masculine and is highly educated compared to the overall population of Ghana

Although certain studies point to an increasing feminisation of the Ghanaian emigrant population – with women moving independently as skilled workers, entrepreneurs and traders – the gender composition of the Ghanaian diaspora in OECD countries has remained practically stable over the last 15 years. In 2015/16, women accounted for 47% of the Ghanaian emigrant population in the OECD area. Women appear to dominate short-distance corridors. They account for the majority of Ghanaian migrant stocks in the neighbouring countries for which data are available, such as Benin, Burkina Faso and Togo.

Approximately a third of the Ghanaian diaspora has achieved tertiary education. English-speaking destinations – the United States, the United Kingdom and Canada – tend to attract more highly educated emigrants. Given its educational and age distribution, the Ghanaian diaspora evidences a positive self-selection among the highly educated and individuals of working age. Conversely, almost 90% of the Ghanaian emigrant population in Ghana's neighbouring countries has achieved a low level of education.

Ghana has the sixth-highest emigration rate among the ECOWAS countries

Ghanaian emigrants represent approximately 3% of the country's total population. The emigration rate to OECD countries is 2.3% (2.1% for women), almost on par with the ECOWAS average (2.1%). The emigration rate, however, is significantly higher among the tertiary educated (14%).

Ghanaian emigrants fare relatively well in OECD labour markets, but substantial variation exists across destination countries

In 2015/16, over three-quarters of the Ghanaian emigrant population of working age participated in OECD labour markets. Overall, the insertion of Ghanaian emigrants into the labour market is comparatively better than among emigrants from other ECOWAS countries. Yet, the situation varies across destination countries with the highest employment rates observed in English-speaking countries. In the United States – the main destination of Ghanaian emigrants in the OECD area – nearly 80% of Ghanaian emigrants were employed in 2017/19. Conversely, in Italy and Germany, employment rates among Ghanaian emigrants were only slightly over 50%. Ghanaian male emigrants fare better in the labour market than women: in 2015/16 their employment rate (75%) was 11 percentage points higher than that of their female counterparts. This gender employment gap, however, remained lower than the gap observed among the native and foreign-born populations of OECD countries.

Employment returns to education are high for Ghanaian emigrants but vary across destination countries

Across OECD countries, the participation of Ghanaian emigrants in the labour market increases with their level of education. The employment rate for the highly educated is 28 percentage points higher than for the low educated, but there is substantial variation across destination countries. Higher employment rates among the tertiary educated hide a significant mismatch between the qualifications of Ghanaian migrants and their occupations in OECD countries: 43% of tertiary-educated migrants from Ghana were overqualified in their occupation. A third of Ghanaian emigrants in the OECD area held an elementary occupation in 2015/16.

In English-speaking countries, Ghanaian emigrants are overrepresented in health-related occupations

A particular feature of the integration of Ghanaian migrants into the labour market is their high participation in health-related occupations, particularly in English-speaking countries. In 2015/16, 5 800 Ghanaian emigrants worked as health professionals in the United Kingdom, which accounts for 9% of the total Ghana-born population of working age living there. Likewise, in the United States, 29% of the Ghana-born labour force was employed in health-related occupations (2017/2019). In Canada, in 2015/16, 11% of Ghanaian emigrants were employed in health-related positions, of which 59% were health professionals. Ghana ranks among the top 20 origin countries of nurses working in the OECD area, a phenomenon that has been amply documented in the literature.

1 Recent trends in emigration from Ghana

This chapter examines recent trends in emigration from Ghana to the main OECD destination countries. In order to better understand the recent evolution in emigration flows, the chapter first traces the historical context of emigration from Ghana since its independence. The following section examines recent migration flows from Ghana to the main OECD destination countries and analyses the nature of these flows, using data on categories of residence permits issued to Ghanaian nationals. Finally, the last section examines emigration intentions among the Ghanaian population and the main determining factors of the desire to emigrate.

In Brief

Key findings

- Migration flows from Ghana to OECD countries are the second highest among the member countries of the Economic Community of West African States (ECOWAS), after Nigeria.

- Migration flows from Ghana to OECD countries have grown slower than other ECOWAS countries, but annual legal migration flows from Ghana more than doubled between 2000 and 2019 (from 12 900 in 2000 to 23 000 in 2008, and to 27 400 in 2019).

- Among OECD countries, the United States attracts the most significant annual flows from Ghana, with more than 8 400 Ghanaian migrating to the country in 2019, followed by the United Kingdom, Italy and Spain. Between 2000 and 2019, these four countries received, on average, 85% of Ghanaian annual flows to OECD countries.

- Men are overrepresented in migration flows from Ghana to the main OECD destination countries, except in the United States.

- Since 2010, more than half of residence permits issued annually to Ghanaian nationals by European countries have been issued for family reasons; one-third have been issued for humanitarian reasons.

- Most permits issued by the United Kingdom to Ghanaian nationals are issued for family reasons, but this country also grants a substantial number of permits for education purposes.

- Forty-four percent of Ghanaians express the intention to emigrate permanently. This share is the third highest among the ECOWAS countries after Sierra Leone (61%) and Liberia (58%). On average, 36% of the ECOWAS population and 37% of the Sub-Saharan African population expressed a desire to emigrate.

- However, these intentions rarely materialise in the short or medium term: only 17% of Ghanaians intending to emigrate consider doing so within a year.

- Emigration intentions are substantially higher among young (56%) and unemployed individuals (58%). The employment situation – characterised by high unemployment rates and a mismatch between education and employment – is the primary driver of emigration intentions in Ghana.

Historical context of Ghanaian emigration

Ghana's history of migration dates back to the pre-colonial period. As the first Sub-Saharan African country to gain independence in 1957 and due to its relative affluence, Ghana became a major destination country for migrants within West Africa through the first part of the 1960s (Schans et al., 2013[1]). During that period, immigration to Ghana stemmed from economic and political factors. The dynamism of the plantations and mining industry led to higher wages and employment opportunities, which attracted large numbers of immigrants from neighbouring countries. Politically, Kwame Nkrumah's foreign policy promoted pan-Africanism, thereby encouraging immigration to Ghana. Therefore, according to the 1960 census, immigrants accounted for 12% of the population in Ghana (IOM, 2019[2]). Emigration, minimal throughout the early 1960s, mostly involved students and professionals pursuing further education and employment opportunities, mainly in the United Kingdom. Some Ghanaian emigrants also migrated to African countries such as Gambia, Botswana, Sierra Leone, Benin, and Côte d'Ivoire to work in public services (Anarfi, Ofosu-Mensah and Ababio, 2017[3]).

These trends began to reverse in the mid-1960s. From 1965, Ghana's attractiveness declined as the country went through an unprecedented economic crisis with growing unemployment and poverty rates, and political instability. The scenario resulted in the international emigration of Ghanaian and foreign nationals. This emigration wave was mostly characterised by labour migration from Ghana to other African countries, such as Nigeria or Côte d'Ivoire (IOM, 2019[2]). Emigrants were mostly professionals – teachers, lawyers, and administrators. Those who had left to pursue their studies abroad and came back to Ghana started leaving the country again and Ghanaian students abroad increasingly stayed in their host country to work (Anarfi, Ofosu-Mensah and Ababio, 2017[3]). The creation of the Economic Community of West African States (ECOWAS) in 1975 and its 1979 Protocol related to the free movement of persons accelerated migration outflows within the region (ICMPD/IOM, 2015[4]). At the same time, Côte d'Ivoire experienced strong economic growth and progressively became the first destination country for emigrants in West Africa.

An intensification in migration outflows and a diversification in destination countries characterised Ghana's third phase of emigration. In addition, the nature of the flows changed, as emigration was no longer restrained to skilled professionals exclusively. In the early 1980s, unskilled Ghanaians began to emigrate en masse from the south of Ghana to neighbouring countries. The implementation of Structural Adjustment Programmes, coupled with a severe period of drought in 1981-82, further caused high unemployment, inflation, and poverty levels prompting significant emigration flows from all sectors of society. Ghanaian nationals migrated to traditional African and English-speaking destinations but also to new destination countries in Europe, North America, South Africa, the Middle East, and North Africa (Schans et al., 2013[1]). In addition, in 1983 and 1985, Nigeria expulsed more than 1.2 million Ghanaians who, for the most part, migrated to other countries (Schans et al., 2013[1]).

International emigration continued throughout the 1990s. A true Ghanaian diaspora was established in main destination countries such as the United Kingdom, the United States, Germany, Italy and, more recently, the Netherlands. If highly skilled migrants tended to migrate to English-speaking countries, unskilled Ghanaians mainly migrated to Italy or Germany. In the 1990s and the early 2000s, the emigration of health professionals to the United States, the United Kingdom and Canada, rapidly increased and quickly became a cause for concern given the growing shortages in the Ghanaian medical sector (IOM, 2011[5]).

Recent migration flows to OECD countries

Ghana is the second ECOWAS country with the highest migration flows to the OECD area

Migration flows from Ghana to OECD countries are the second highest among the countries of the Economic Community of West African States (ECOWAS), after Nigeria. Migration flows from Ghana reached 27 400 persons in 2019, according to the *OECD International Migration Database* (Annex A), while flows from Nigeria were roughly 71 000 that same year. Since 2000, the volume of flows from Ghana has been relatively close to Senegal's and higher than the volume of flows from Guinea, Côte d'Ivoire and Mali (Figure 1.1).

If the annual number of Ghanaian nationals migrating to the OECD area has been higher than for most ECOWAS countries, the growth in migration flows has been slower. Among ECOWAS countries, Ghana ranked tenth in terms of the growth rate of migration flows between 2000 and 2019. During the first decade, flows from Ghana to OECD countries increased by 79%, while flows from Guinea, Benin, Gambia, Mali and Burkina Faso rose by over 300%, and flows from Nigeria, Senegal, and Côte d'Ivoire grew by more than 100%. The growth in migration flows from Ghana was even lower between 2010 and 2019 (19%).

However, emigration from Ghana, especially to the OECD area, is an older phenomenon than some ECOWAS countries. In 2000, Ghana's volume of migration flows was already higher than other West African countries except for Nigeria. Yet, annual migration flows from Ghana to OECD countries more than doubled between 2000 and 2019, from 12 900 in 2000 to 23 000 in 2008, and to 27 400 in 2019 (Figure 1.2).

The *OECD International Migration Database* data refer to the annual legal migration flows from Ghana to OECD countries. Although there are irregular migration flows from Ghana, it is very difficult to measure them. There are no reliable and comparable data available on irregular entries of foreign nationals in OECD countries. Migrants who legally entered destination countries and later become irregular can hardly be identified. Therefore, the data on actual migration flows to OECD countries and the number of Ghanaian emigrants might be underestimated.

Figure 1.1. Annual migration flows from selected ECOWAS countries to OECD countries, by nationality, 2000-19

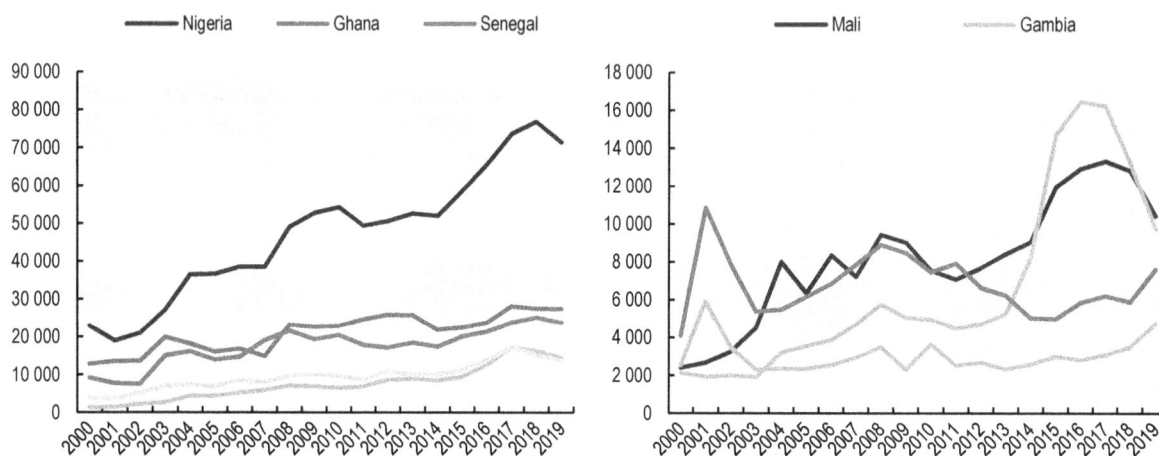

Source: OECD International Migration Database (2021).

Figure 1.2. Migration flows from Ghana to OECD countries, 2000-19

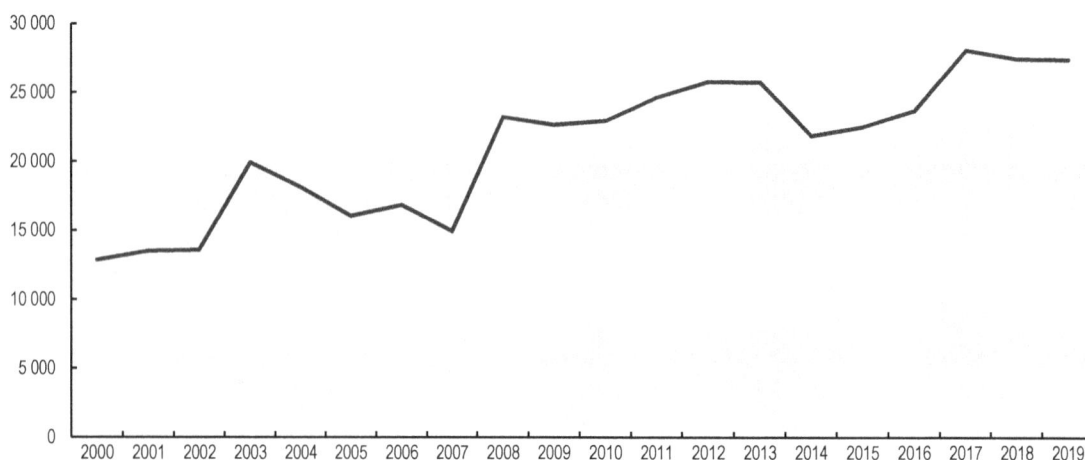

Note: All figures are obtained as the sum of standardised gross flows for countries where they are available.
Source: OECD International Migration Database (2021). Data on flows to the United Kingdom come from Eurostat (2020), "First permits by reason, length of validity and citizenship".

The United States attracts the largest flows of Ghanaian nationals

On an average yearly basis, the United States, Germany, the United Kingdom, Italy, and Spain received 85% of Ghanaian nationals immigrating to OECD countries between 2000 and 2019. In the OECD area, the United States has by far attracted the largest annual flows of Ghanaian nationals since 2000, with more than 8 400 Ghanaian migrating to the country in 2019 (Figure 1.3). Flows to the United States substantially grew between 2000 and 2006 (by 115%) reaching roughly 9 400 Ghanaians by 2006, and peaking at more than 10 500 in 2012. After a decline, flows have stagnated at around 8 400 since 2017. In 2019, flows from Ghana to the United States were among the highest of all African countries after Nigeria and Egypt.

The United Kingdom has historically been one of the leading destination countries for Ghanaian emigrants. As detailed above, the highly skilled migration of Ghanaians to the United Kingdom gradually expanded following Ghana's independence. Between 2000 and 2019, flows to the United Kingdom more than tripled, peaking at 7 000 in 2003 and 6 000 in 2011.

Flows from Ghana to Germany and Italy have increased over the past decade, reflecting a diversification in destination countries. Flows to Italy even somewhat exceeded those to the United Kingdom over the recent years (Figure 1.3). The number of Ghanaian nationals arriving in Italy rose by 66% between 2000 and 2008. It further grew between 2014 and 2017, when almost 4 500 Ghanaian nationals migrated to the country. Similarly, flows to Germany increased almost five-fold between 2008 and 2019 (close to 5 000 persons in 2019).

Figure 1.3. Migration flows from Ghana to main OECD destination countries, 2000-19

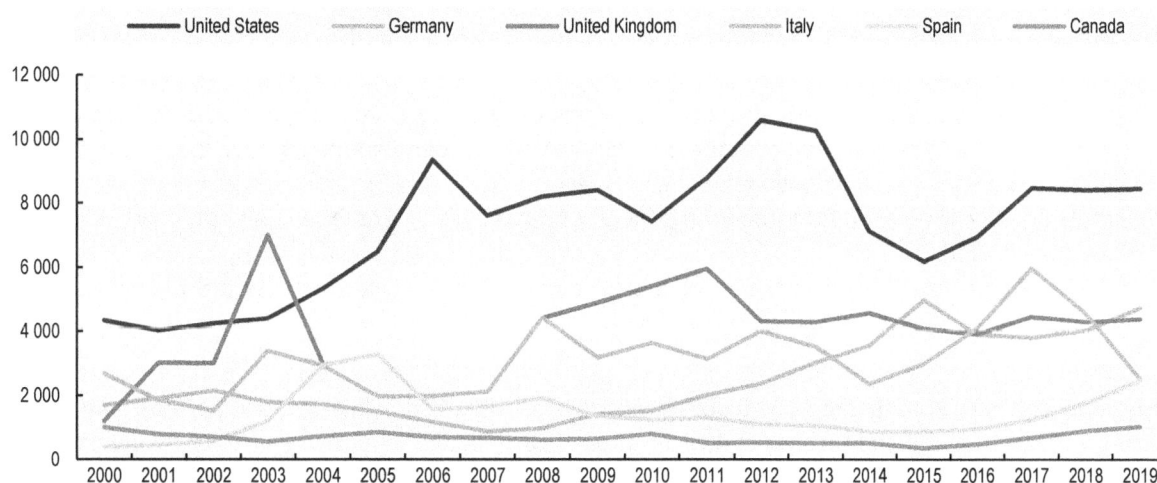

Note: Data on flows to the United Kingdom are not available between 2005 and 2007. Flows to the United Kingdom in 2019 are an estimation. Source: OECD International Migration Database (2021). Data on flows to the United Kingdom come from Eurostat (2020), "First permits by reason, length of validity and citizenship" (2020).

Overall, men are overrepresented in migration flows from Ghana to the main OECD destination countries. The share of men among is especially high in Italy (59%) and Germany (56%). Conversely, women are slightly overrepresented in migration flows to the United States, representing 54% of Ghanaian nationals migrating to the United States in 2019. Regarding flows to Canada and the Netherlands, slightly more than half of Ghanaian nationals in 2019 were men.

Figure 1.4. Share of women and men in migration flows from Ghana to main OECD destination countries, 2019

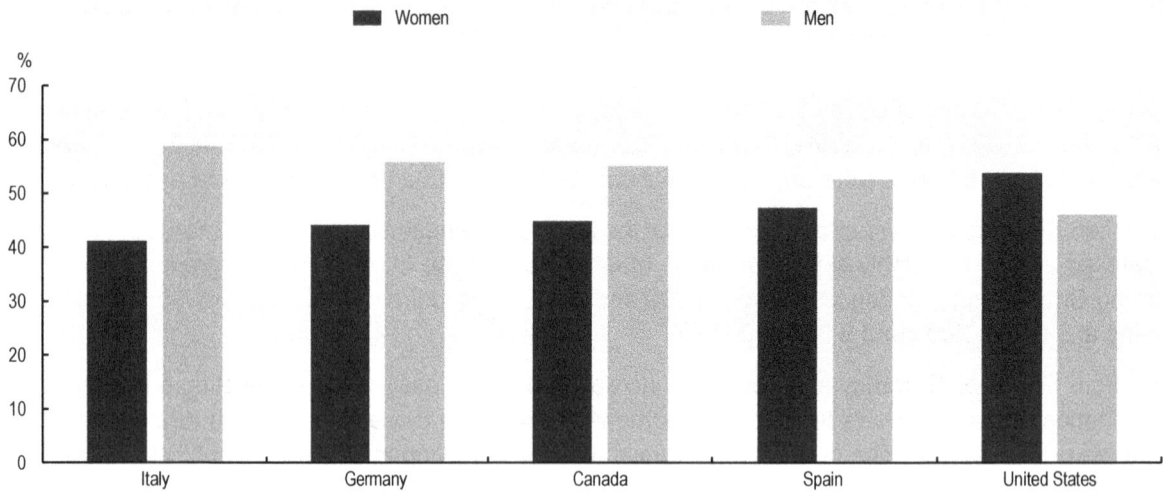

Note: Data for the United Kingdom are not available.
Source: Eurostat (2020), "First permits by reason, age, sex and citizenship", and International Migration Database (2020). For Canada and the United States: OECD International Migration Database (2021).

Categories of residence permits issued to Ghanaian nationals by OECD countries

The data collected by Eurostat on first residence permits issued by European countries to third-country nationals (see Annex A) reveals that over the past ten years, European countries have issued the majority of residence permits to Ghanaian nationals for family reasons (Figure 1.5). On average, between 2016 and 2020, family permits accounted for more than 50% of all permits issued to Ghanaian nationals, while 32% of permits were issued for "other" reasons – a category including mostly permits for humanitarian reasons, 13% for education reasons, and only 6% for work reasons. Family based permits are mainly issued to Ghanaian children and spouses joining non-EU citizens.

This distribution evolved over time: the number of first permits delivered to Ghanaian nationals for professional reasons sharply fell from 6 500 in 2010 to 770 in 2015, while the number of humanitarian permits increased, accounting for almost 40% of all permits issued to Ghanaians in 2017. This share then decreased, reaching 10% in 2020. In contrast, the share of permits issued for education remained relatively steady, averaging around 13% of all permits between 2010 and 2020.

Figure 1.5. Residence permits issued by European countries to Ghanaian nationals by reason, 2010-20

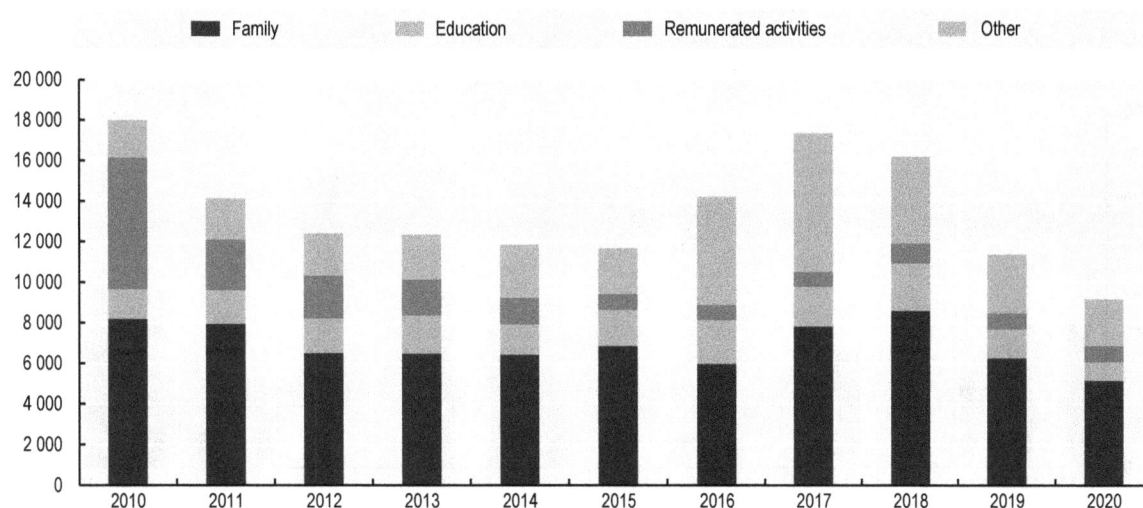

Note: The data correspond to the first residence permits issued to Ghanaian nationals for all durations.
Source: Eurostat (2020), "First permits by reason, length of validity and citizenship", (database).

The nature of migration flows from Ghana to OECD countries varies across destination countries. The data collected by the United States Office of Immigration Statistics indicate that the majority of permanent residence permits for Ghanaian nationals in 2019 were issued for family reasons. More specifically, most of these permanent permits were issued to immediate relatives of the United States citizens. In addition, the United States also issues a substantial number of non-immigrant temporary permits to Ghanaian nationals, among which 70% are student permits and 20% are issued to temporary workers and families.

As highlighted in Figure 1.6, Germany almost exclusively issued permits for family and humanitarian reasons to Ghanaian nationals between 2010 and 2020. In 2010, permits for family reasons accounted for 74% of all permits issued by Germany. This share decreased over time as the number of permits issued for humanitarian reasons rose. The latter accounted for 18 to 24% of all permits between 2010 and 2018, but reached 43% in 2020. Therefore, data suggest that migration flows to Germany are driven marginally by education and professional reasons.

Most permits issued by the United Kingdom to Ghanaian nationals are also for family reasons. However, the United Kingdom is the only main European destination country to grant a substantial number of permits for education purposes to Ghanaian nationals. This trend can be explained by knowledge of the English language among the Ghanaian population, historical ties, and the perceived quality of the British education system. On average, almost one in five residence permit issued to Ghanaian nationals by the United Kingdom were issued for education reasons. Conversely, only 2% of permits issued by Italy and Spain, and 7%of permits issued by Germany were for education purposes (Figure 1.6).

In the early 2010s, Italy granted most residence permits to Ghanaian nationals for work reasons. While this share gradually decreased, the number of permits for humanitarian reasons increased in 2015 and peaked at 4 500 in 2017 (72%). Therefore, the overall increase in the share of permits for humanitarian reasons issued by European countries to Ghanaian nationals in 2016 and 2017 is mainly attributable to the increase in Italy, and a lesser extent, in the United Kingdom.

The increase in the issuance of permits for humanitarian reasons by Italy to Ghanaian nationals coincides with a surge in first-time asylum applicants in 2016 and 2017. Between 2013 and 2017, the number of Ghanaian asylum claims in Italy grew ten-fold to reach almost 5 000 claims in 2017 (Annex Figure 1.A.1). The number of Ghanaian asylum applicants from Germany also peaked in 2016 (2 600 claims).

Figure 1.6. Residence permits issued to Ghanaian nationals by Germany, Italy and the United Kingdom, by reason, 2010-20

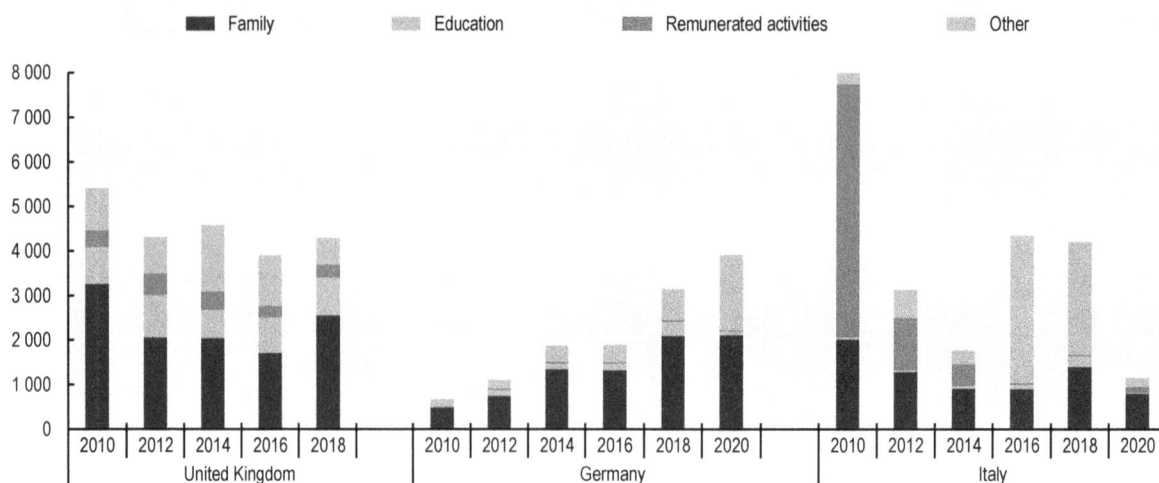

Note: Data correspond to the first residence permits issued to Ghanaian nationals for all durations.
Source: Eurostat (2020), "First permits by reason, length of validity and citizenship" (database).

Women are more likely to receive permits for family reasons than men are. As highlighted in Figure 1.7, in 2019, over 60% of permits issued to Ghanaian women by all European OECD countries were family permits, while they accounted for only 38% of permits issued to men. This gap is especially pronounced for permits issued by Spain and Italy: 90% and 87% of Ghanaian women received family permits in Italy and Spain, respectively, compared to about half of men in 2019. Furthermore, in every main European destination country, men are more likely to receive humanitarian permits: 46% of Ghanaian men received humanitarian permits in 2019, while only 29% of women did.

Figure 1.7. Residence permits issued to Ghanaian nationals by main European destination countries, by reason and sex, 2019

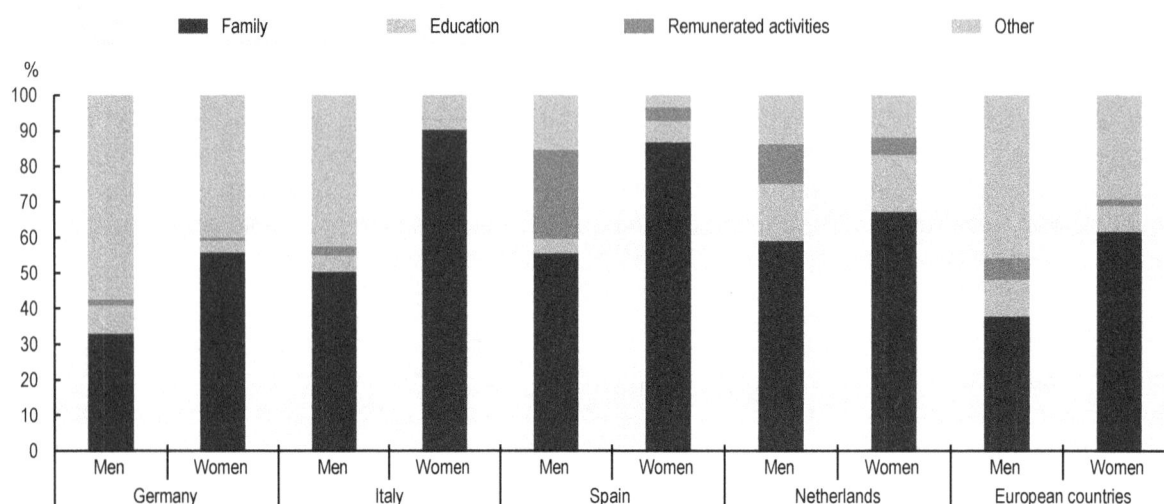

Note: Data for the United Kingdom are not available.
Source: Eurostat (2020), "First permits by reason, age, sex and citizenship" (database).

Box 1.1. Migration from Ghana to West Africa and other non-OECD countries

The Economic Community of West African States (ECOWAS) was created in 1975 with the ratification of the Treaty of Lagos to promote and ensure economic and political co-operation and integration between member states. Between 1979 and 1993, six protocols established, among other things, the right of entry, the abolition of visa requirements for stays lasting less than 90 days, and the right of residence within ECOWAS member countries (ICMPD/IOM, 2015[4]). A large share of migration flows from Ghana take place within the African continent, especially in the ECOWAS zone. However, data on migration flows in Africa are scarce, making it difficult to quantify annual migration flows from Ghana to other African countries. In 2018, almost 42% of all migrants from ECOWAS countries went to other ECOWAS member states. Of the emigration flows out of the ECOWAS region, 23% went to other African countries, 23% to the European Union, and 14% to North America. Migration flows between ECOWAS countries are mainly driven by labour and humanitarian reasons (ICMPD/IOM, 2015[4]). These migrations are primarily temporary, seasonal and short-term cross-border movements. The largest migration corridor involving Ghana in West Africa is that from Ghana to Nigeria (IOM, 2020[6])

The COVID-19 pandemic and the restrictions imposed globally have caused a considerable decrease in migration flows. The International Organisation for Migration (IOM) has estimated that migration flows within West and Central Africa were reduced by 48% between 2019 and the first half of 2020. In June 2020, it was estimated that more than 30 000 migrants were stranded at borders. Nevertheless, despite the health restrictions, migration flows continued for some categories of migrants who moved irregularly (IOM, 2020[6]).

Recent intensification of migration flows of Ghanaian domestic workers to the Middle East

National data on migration flows from Ghana show that flows of Ghanaian nationals to Middle Eastern countries have significantly increased over the past 20 years. The rapid growth in the number of employment agencies recruiting Ghanaian migrant domestic workers to work abroad primarily contributed to this increase (IOM, 2019[7]). The main destination countries in this region are Saudi Arabia, Qatar, Jordan and Kuwait (IOM, 2019[2]). In 2016, about 2 400 Ghanaian workers were recruited to work in those four countries. Other countries in the Middle East are also important destinations: Lebanon issued 2000 permits to Ghanaian workers in 2017 (IOM, 2019[7]). If flows from Ghana to the Gulf States are mainly composed of women domestic workers, some Ghanaian nationals migrating to the Middle East are also employed as labourers and steel fixers.

Emigration prospects among the Ghanaian population

Data on emigration intentions among the population living in Ghana provide a better understanding of the scope and drivers of Ghanaian emigration flows. Furthermore, emigration intentions can provide valuable insights into future trends in these flows. The Gallup World Poll (see Annex A) collects information on the emigration intentions of persons born and residing in Ghana aged 15 years or older. Data on the characteristics of these individuals make it possible to analyse correlations between intentions to leave the country and various socio-economic variables such as education level and employment status.

Intentions to emigrate from Ghana are high relative to other ECOWAS countries

Between 2009 and 2018, 44% of persons born and living in Ghana aged 15 or older expressed the intention to emigrate (Figure 1.8). This share is one of the highest among ECOWAS countries after Sierra Leone (61%) and Liberia (58%). An average of 36% of persons living in the ECOWAS region and 37% of those living in Sub-Saharan Africa indicated a wish to emigrate. If intentions to emigrate in Nigeria, Togo and Gambia were only slightly lower than in Ghana, emigration intentions in Benin (29%), Burkina Faso (27%), Mali (20%), and Niger (16%) were significantly lower. The reported favourite destinations of Ghanaians intending to migrate in 2018 were the United States (28%), the United Kingdom (14%), Germany (9%), and Canada (6%). These countries reflect Ghanaian nationals' actual main OECD destination countries in 2018. However, although they rank fourth and fifth in terms of annual flows from Ghana to OECD countries, Ghanaians rarely designate Italy and Spain as desired destinations (only 2% and 1%, respectively). Similarly, only 2% of Ghanaians indicated Nigeria as their favourite destination, whereas flows from Ghana to Nigeria have been and remain substantial. Therefore, these countries seem to represent more of a step in the migration experience than destination countries where Ghanaian emigrants intend to settle permanently.

Figure 1.8. Emigration intentions in ECOWAS countries, 2009-18

Share of the population (aged 15 years and over) born and living in the country who consider emigrating permanently

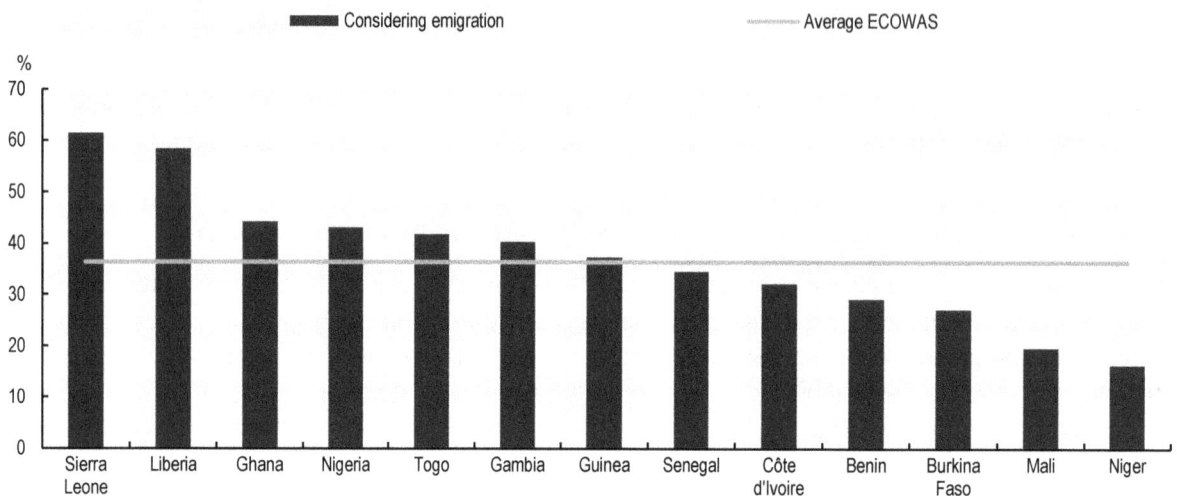

Note: Considering emigration means answering "yes" to: "Ideally, if you had the opportunity, would you like to live permanently in another country?"
Source: Gallup World Poll (2021).

However, these intentions rarely materialise in the short or medium term. The question "Do you plan to move permanently to another country in the next 12 months" included in the Gallup survey makes it possible to assess whether the desire to emigrate is likely to be translated into action within a defined period. The responses to this question reveal, for Ghana and every ECOWAS country, a significant gap between the intention to emigrate and the probability of this intention materialising in the short term. While 44% of Ghanaians wish to emigrate, only 17% of them considered doing so within a year. This share is the lowest out of all ECOWAS countries except for Nigeria, where only 10% of people considering emigration indicate a wish to leave the country within a year.

Emigration intentions are especially high among young and unemployed Ghanaians

Emigration intentions vary significantly according to socio-demographic characteristics such as age, education level, and labour market status. In Ghana and other ECOWAS countries, emigration intentions are particularly high among young people. On average, between 2009 and 2018, 47% of people aged 15-24 living in ECOWAS countries wished to leave the country permanently. This share in Ghana is even higher: more than half of young Ghanaians (56%) indicated considering emigration, a share that is 12 percentage points higher than that recorded in the total population. However, very few planned to leave the country within the next 12 months (17%). Intentions to emigrate further vary across genders: in Ghana, 48% of men said they would like to emigrate, while 40% of women did.

As expected, emigration intentions also differ according to labour market status: 58% of self-reported unemployed individuals expressed the desire to leave the country against 41% of employed individuals and 46% of individuals out of the workforce. Education levels also influence the desire to emigrate. Individuals with high or intermediate education are more likely to express an intention to emigrate compared to low-skilled individuals: 54% of Ghanaians with an intermediate education level and 41% of those highly educated express the wish to emigrate, while 37% of those with low education levels declare an intention to emigrate.

High unemployment and a low labour force participation rate characterise the labour market situation of young people in Ghana. As the young population and the number of highly educated individuals in Ghana grew increasingly faster, employment opportunities have lagged. This gap between educational attainment and the labour market has triggered high unemployment rates among young people, especially tertiary graduates (Dako-Gyeke, 2016[8]). Therefore, the significant mismatch between labour supply and demand and the difficulty for Ghanaians with an intermediate or high education level to find a job matching their qualifications and aspirations may push them to consider seeking a better situation abroad.

However, intentions to emigrate do not always correspond to actual emigration decisions, especially for certain demographic groups. Employed or skilled people are likely to possess higher economic and social capital necessary to emigrate than the young or unemployed, who face more difficulties concretely contemplating emigration.

Figure 1.9. Emigration intentions among various groups in Ghana, 2009-18

Share of the population (aged 15 years and over) born in the country who consider emigrating permanently

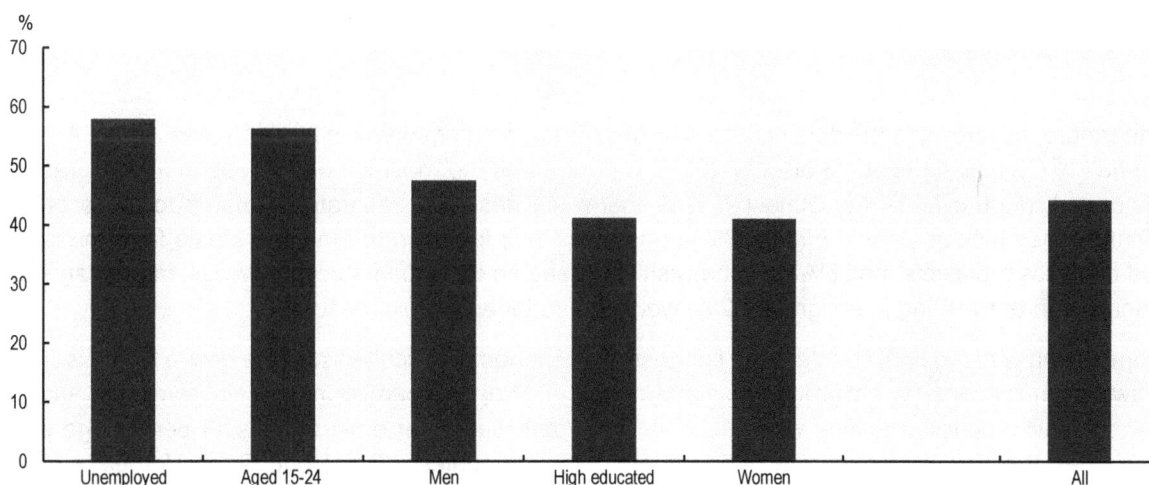

Note: High education refers to at least four years of completed education beyond high school, or a four-year college degree.
Source: Gallup World Poll (2021).

The employment situation seems to be the main driver of emigration intentions in Ghana

Available data on the subjective well-being of Ghanaians who wish to emigrate shed light on the determinants of emigration intentions and, indirectly, on the factors that drive actual migration flows. The majority of the overall Ghanaian population reported having difficulties living on their current income and being unsatisfied with the availability of good jobs. Only 55% of people considering emigration declared that their current job was ideal, compared to 68% of Ghanaians who did not wish to leave the country (Figure 1.10). Furthermore, individuals considering emigration are slightly more likely to be unsatisfied with the availability of good jobs than those who do not consider emigrating. In addition, those expressing a desire to emigrate are more likely to have a network of friends or family to rely on abroad: 35% of them declared being able to count on those networks outside the country, against 30% of those who do not wish to emigrate.

Figure 1.10. Emigration intentions and opinions of persons born and living in Ghana, 2009-18

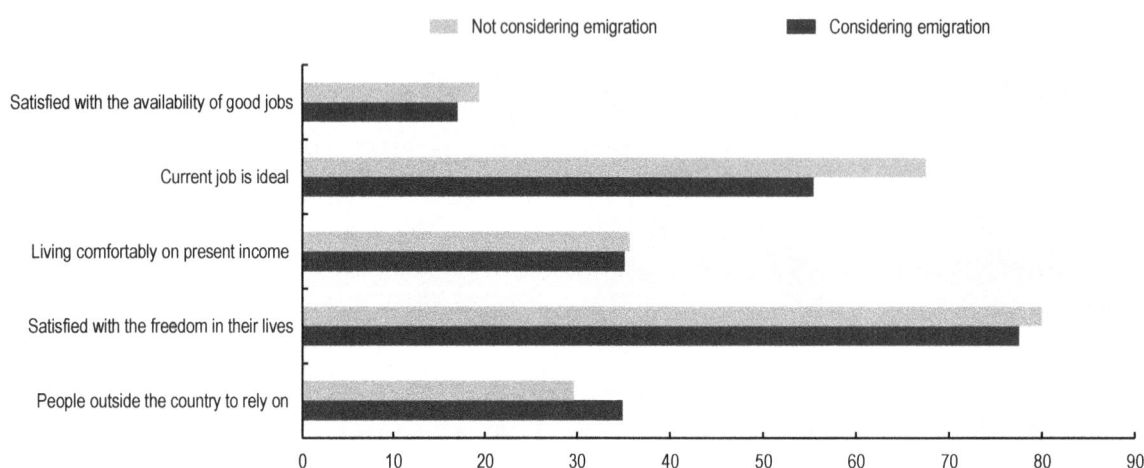

Note: Data on the availability of good jobs and whether the current job is ideal are only available between 2010 and 2012.
Source: Gallup World Poll (2021).

Furthermore, according to the data collected by the Afrobarometer survey in 2016/18 (see Annex A), more than half of Ghanaians aged 18 or older (53%) reported that the most important reason for emigrating is to find work (Figure 1.11). For almost 20% of them, the desire to emigrate is related to the economic difficulties they face in Ghana. Finally, 8% argued that their intention to emigrate stems from the lack of good business prospects, and 6% from the wish to pursue an education abroad. Overall, more than seven Ghanaians in ten wishing to emigrate (72%) would do so for economic reasons.

A comparison with regional counterparts suggests that economic difficulties and the desire to find work are the two main reasons for emigration for most people in West African countries. However, the share of Ghanaians who consider finding work the most important reason for emigrating is 11 percentage points higher than the ECOWAS average (42%). Along with Senegalese (54%) and Cabo Verdeans (64%), Ghanaians much more frequently invoked this reason than other populations of ECOWAS countries. It, therefore, seems that the lack of employment opportunities in Ghana is a determining factor in the emigration process.

Figure 1.11. Main reasons for emigrating, 2016/18

Share of the population in Ghana (aged 18 or older) considering emigration

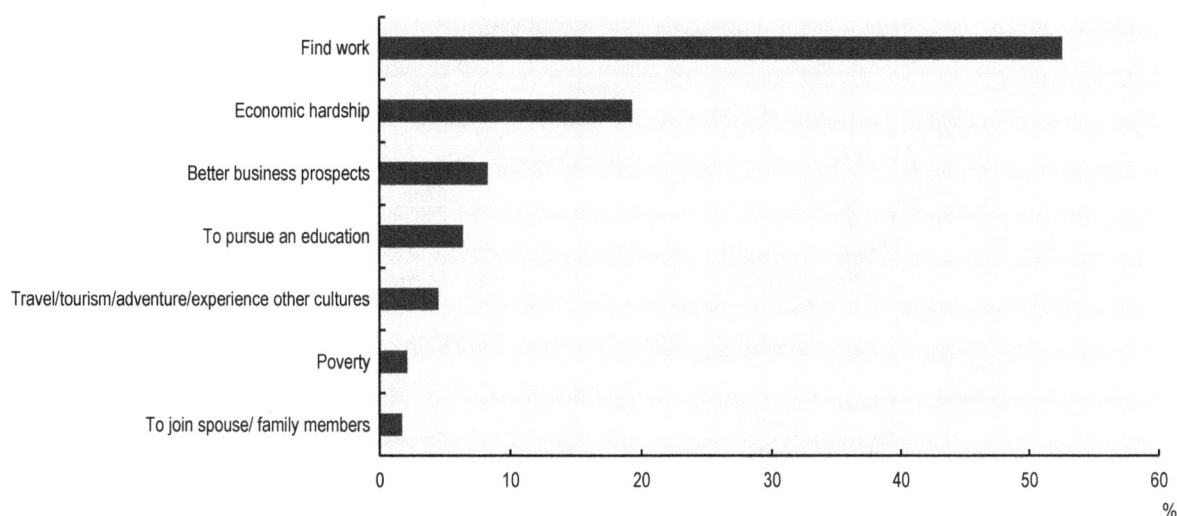

Note: This question is not available for previous survey waves. Answers to the question "There are several reasons why people leave their home to live in another country for an extended period of time. What about you? What is the most important reason why you would consider moving from [country]?" N=992.
Source: Afrobarometer, 2016/2018 survey wave.

Conclusion

Migration flows from Ghana to OECD countries have intensified over the past 20 years. The United States has been, by far, the leading OECD destination country for Ghanaian nationals, followed by the United Kingdom, Germany, Italy and Spain. The majority of residence permits issued annually to Ghanaian nationals are first and foremost issued for family reasons, although the number of permits issued for humanitarian reasons has increased since 2015. The Ghanaian population expresses higher emigration intentions than most West African countries, although these intentions rarely materialise in the short or medium term. The desire to emigrate permanently from Ghana is even higher among young and unemployed individuals. The difficult employment situation is the main driver of emigration intentions in Ghana.

References

Anarfi, J., Ofosu-Mensah and E. Ababio (2017), "A historical perspective from and to Ghana", in *Migration in a Globalizing World*, Sub-Saharan Publishers, https://doi.org/10.2307/j.ctvh8r2m4.8. [3]

Dako-Gyeke, M. (2016), "Exploring the Migration Intentions of Ghanaian Youth: A Qualitative Study", *Journal of International Migration and Integration*, Vol. 17/3, pp. 723-744, https://doi.org/10.1007/s12134-015-0435-z. [8]

ICMPD/IOM (2015), *A Survey on Migration Policies in West Africa*, International Centre for Migration Policy Development, International Organisation for Migrations. [4]

IOM (2020), *Migration Data in West Africa - Regional Data Overview*. [6]

IOM (2019), *Ghana Migration Profile*, International Organisation for Migration. [2]

IOM (2019), *Ghanaian domestic workers in the Middle East*, International Organisation for Migration. [7]

IOM (2011), *National Profile of Migration of Health Professionals – Ghana*, International Organisation for Migration - Migration Health Division. [5]

Schans, D. et al. (2013), "Changing Patterns of Ghanaian Migration", in *Migration between Africa and Europe*, Springer International Publishing, Cham, https://doi.org/10.1007/978-3-319-69569-3_10. [1]

Annex 1.A. Additional figures

Annex Figure 1.A.1. First-time asylum claims by Ghanaian nationals in main European destination countries, 2008-20

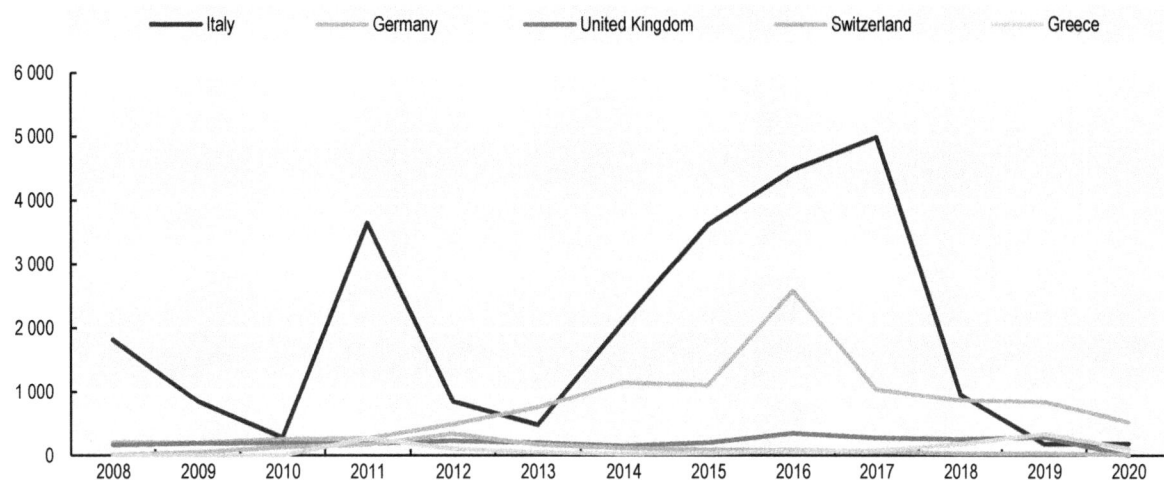

Source: Eurostat (2021), "Asylum applicants by type of applicant, citizenship, age and sex", (database).

2 Number of Ghanaian emigrants and their socio-demographic characteristics

This chapter examines the size of the Ghanaian diaspora in the main destination countries, and its evolution since 2000. It provides a socio-demographic analysis, focusing on age and educational distribution, emphasising differences by sex and across destination countries. For the central destination countries, it provides a snapshot of the geographic distribution of emigrants, and information on the acquisition of nationality. The chapter also presents evidence on the overall emigration rates of the Ghanaian population and its highly educated population towards OECD countries. The analysis systematically compares the Ghanaian diaspora with two reference groups: the foreign-born population living in the OECD area and emigrants from the Economic Community of West African States (ECOWAS).

In Brief

- In 2020, approximately 1 million Ghanaian emigrants were living abroad, with almost an equal distribution in African and OECD countries. In Africa, Ghanaian emigrants are mostly concentrated in the ECOWAS area, and Nigeria alone hosts a quarter of the overall diaspora. In the OECD area, five countries – the United States, the United Kingdom, Italy, Germany and Canada – account for almost 90% of the Ghanaian emigrant population.

- National estimates of the Ghanaian diaspora are not only outdated – the last census data currently available is from 2010 – but significantly lower than those reported in other sources.

- The Ghanaian refugee population of about 14 000 is highly concentrated in neighbouring Togo. While the number of refugees has remained relatively stable in recent years, the number of asylum seekers increased 10-fold between 2010 and 2020.

- In 2019, approximately 9 000 Ghanaian students were enrolled in a tertiary-level institution abroad. Nine out of ten were studying in an OECD country with a preference for English-speaking countries: the United States hosts more than a third of Ghanaian international students.

- Women comprise 47% of the Ghanaian diaspora in OECD countries. Conversely, in the African countries for which there is data available, Ghanaian women represent the majority of stocks.

- Eight out of ten Ghanaian emigrants in OECD countries are of working age, a higher share than the total foreign-born population.

- In 2015/16, more than a third of Ghanaian migrants living in OECD countries had tertiary education, reflecting a strong positive selection of emigrants to the OECD area. The share of tertiary-educated migrants from Ghana is higher in English-speaking countries. Lower-educated emigrants predominate in Italy and Germany.

- Almost half of the Ghanaian emigrants held the citizenship of their OECD host country in 2015/16.

- In 2015, Ghana had an emigration rate towards OECD countries of 2.3%, the sixth-highest among the ECOWAS countries, and 14% among its highly educated population.

Recent trends in the number of Ghanaian emigrants

One million Ghanaian emigrants live abroad: about half in other African countries and half in OECD countries

According to United Nations estimates, approximately 1 million Ghanaian emigrants lived abroad in 2020, 3.2% of Ghana's population. This diaspora is distributed almost equally between OECD countries – mainly in North America and Europe (close to 52% of the Ghanaian emigrant population) – and sub-Saharan Africa (48%) (Figure 2.1). In Africa, the Ghanaian diaspora is primarily concentrated in the ECOWAS area, which hosts 46% of all Ghanaian emigrants worldwide.

According to UN estimates, Nigeria is the leading destination country, accounting for 24% of all Ghanaian emigrants (approximately 238 000 emigrants). In sub-Saharan Africa, Nigeria is followed by Ghana's neighbouring countries: Côte d'Ivoire (112 000 emigrants), Togo (47 000), and Burkina Faso (33 000) together account for 19% of the Ghanaian diaspora. Outside of the ECOWAS area, South Africa is also a significant African destination for Ghanaian and continental emigrants, more generally. Outside Africa, the United States is the second leading destination country (201 000 emigrants), followed by the United Kingdom (131 000), Italy (55 000), Germany (33 000) and Canada (25 000).

Figure 2.1. Number of Ghanaian emigrants in main destination countries, 2020 or the latest year available

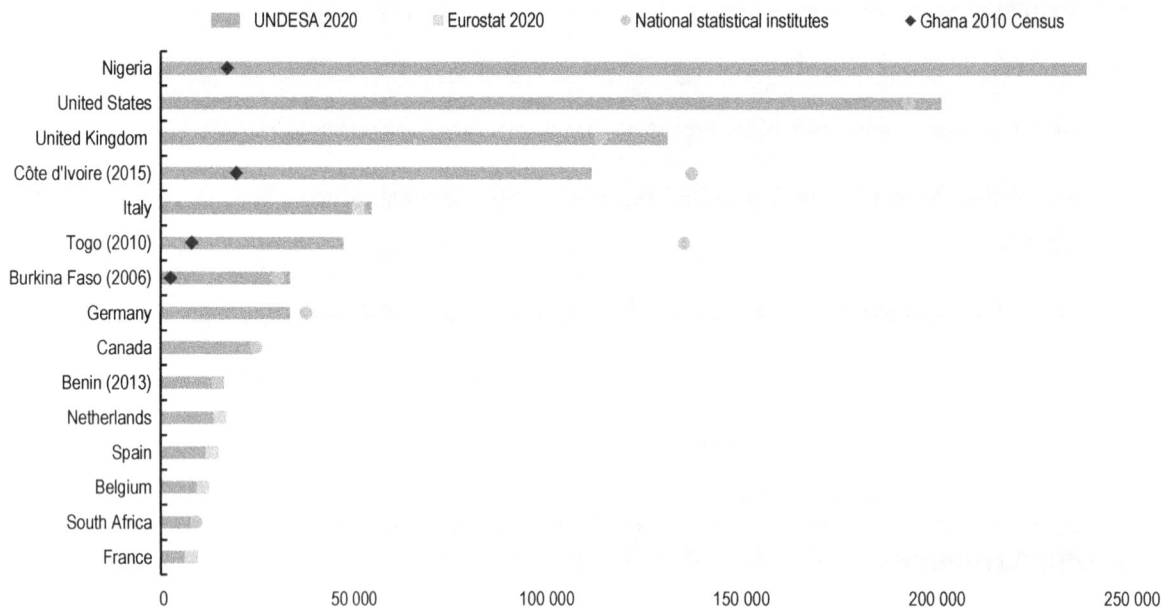

Note: Data from national statistical offices in destination countries come from censuses, registries or household surveys. Where data are prior to 2015, the year is shown in parentheses next to the country name. Côte d'Ivoire, Germany and Italy estimate the Ghanaian population by the country of citizenship, not the country of birth.
Source: United Nations Department of Economic and Social Affairs, Population Division, International Migrant Stock 2020; Benin (2013 Census via IPUMS); Burkina Faso (2006 Census via IPUMS); Canada (2016 Census data); Côte d'Ivoire (2015 General Household Survey); South Africa (2016 Community Survey via IPUMS); Spain (Eurostat 2019); Togo (2010 Census via IPUMS); the United Kingdom (2011 Census); the United States (American Community Survey pooled data for 2017-19); Germany (Central Registry for Foreigners, 2019).

Box 2.2. Ghanaian emigrants and their households in the 2010 Census

Ghana is one of the few countries in the ECOWAS area that collects information on its emigrants through a specific census module. Data from the 2010 Population and Housing Census – the most recent census for which data is currently available – indicated that about 250 000 Ghanaians aged 15 and older had been living abroad for at least six months. Among them, 150 000 were living in North America and Europe. However, these figures underestimate the size of the emigrant population as they rely on information provided by household members in Ghana, thus omitting emigrants who were living alone before emigrating, as well as the departure of entire households. In 2010, the actual number of Ghana-born individuals aged 15 and older living in OECD countries was close to 410 000, almost three times the census estimate.

According to the same data source, about half of Ghanaian emigrants in 2010 came from two regions: Ashanti and Accra, two of Ghana's most populated and urbanised regions (IOM, 2020[1]). Households with emigrants represented approximately 3% of all households in the country. Among the households with emigrants, 71% had only one member abroad, and 16% had two.

The average emigrant was 37 years old, and men represent the majority of stocks (64%), which explains that households in Ghana with at least one emigrant are more likely to be led by women (55%). Once abroad, 76% of Ghanaian emigrants were employed and 14% were studying.

The Ghanaian diaspora makes important contributions to the economic development of their country of origin. In 2020, Ghana received approximately USD 4.3 billion in remittances, which amounts to 6% of its GDP, compared to an ECOWAS average of 7% (Figure 2.2). Between 2010 and 2020, these transfers increased by 32-fold, peaking in 2015 when Ghanaians abroad remitted approximately USD 5 billion. According to officials of the Bank of Ghana, the sharp increase reflects improved statistics by the Bank of Ghana, as well as a rise in both financial transfers and the use of formal channels (Koyi Teye, Badasu and Yeboah, 2017[2]).

Figure 2.2. Personal remittances sent to Ghana, USD million, 2000-20

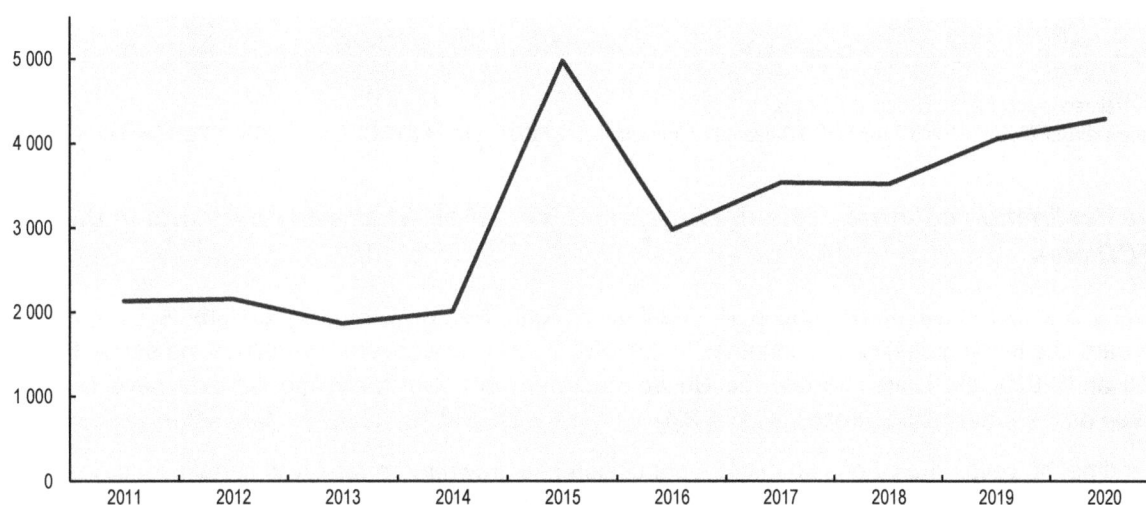

Note: Remittances include workers' remittances and compensation of employees.
Source: IMF Balance of Payments 2020.

Nearly half a million Ghanaian emigrants live in OECD countries

According to the most recent estimates, about 490 000 people born in Ghana lived in OECD countries in 2020 (Figure 2.3). Ghana is the second-largest ECOWAS origin country of emigrants living in the OECD area after Nigeria (with approximately 940 000). In 2020, Ghana represented 8% of the ECOWAS population but accounted for 16% of all emigrants from ECOWAS countries living in the OECD area. The relative preponderance of its emigrant population can be explained by its economic weight within the bloc (the third-highest GDP per capita of the group) and by a history of extra continental migration that dates back to the 1980s. Economic development in developing countries boosts international migration as more people have the financial resources needed to migrate, and consolidated migrant networks contribute to facilitating emigration (OECD, 2016[3]).

Between 2000 and 2020, the number of emigrants from Ghana living in OECD countries registered a 3-fold increase. In absolute terms, such growth (+325 000 persons) ranks second only to Nigeria (+682 000 persons). However, in percentage terms, Ghana ranks among the lower half of the ECOWAS countries (Guinea, Togo, Burkina Faso, Gambia, Côte d'Ivoire, Nigeria, Liberia and Niger), which is primarily explained by a strong base effect for these countries.

Figure 2.3. Number of emigrants from Ghana and ECOWAS countries living in OECD countries, 2000-20

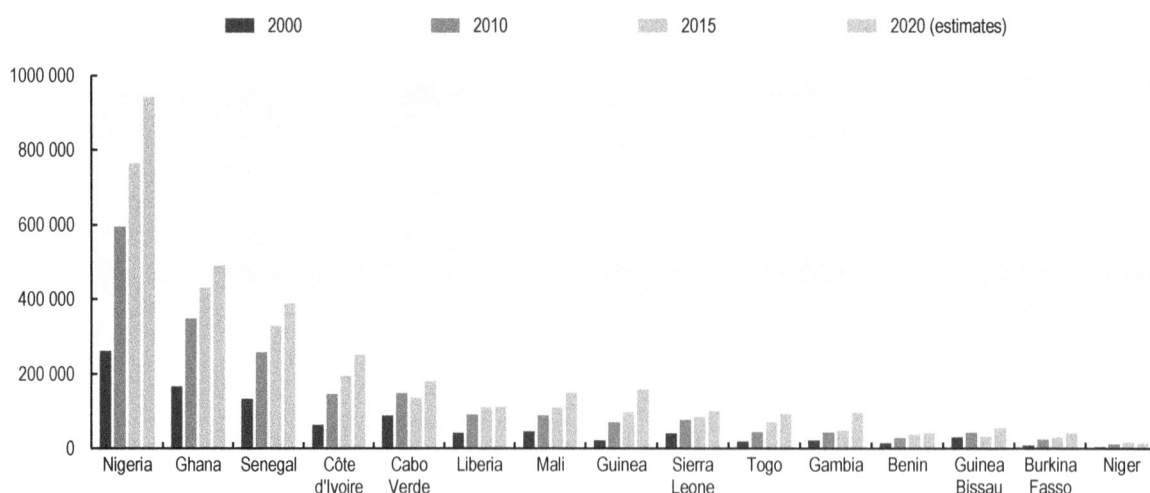

Note: Reference population includes all persons.
Source: Data for 2000, 2010 and 2015: OECD Database on Immigrants in OECD Countries (DIOC). Data for 2020: OECD Secretariat estimates.

Five destination countries account for almost 90% of all Ghanaian emigrants in the OECD area

Despite the increased diversification in destination countries for Ghanaian emigrants over the past 20 years, the leading destination countries in the OECD area have, overall, remained the same. Between 2000 and 2020, the United States, the United Kingdom, Italy, Germany and Canada have constantly ranked as the main host countries (Figure 2.4).

Over time, however, the Ghanaian migrant population has grown more rapidly in certain countries than in others. The United States and the United Kingdom hosted a similar population of Ghanaian migrants at the beginning of the century (62 000 and 53 000, respectively) with a difference of less than 9 000. In 2020, the difference between them had enlarged to approximately 82 000. Since 2000, the Ghanaian diaspora has increased the most in the United States in absolute terms, growing by three-fold (+131 000) to reach almost 200 000 in 2020. The second-largest absolute increase, observed in the United Kingdom, is significantly lower (+58 000).

In percentage terms, Italy has registered the largest growth, although starting at a much lower base due to the relative recency of Ghanaian immigration. From less than 20 000 Ghanaian migrants in 2000, the population grew 3.3 times by 2020 to reach 55 000. In Germany, the fourth destination country, with approximately 37 000 Ghanaian migrants in 2020, the lack of data provides an incomplete picture of the diaspora's evolution. However, between 2010 and 2020, this population increased 1.5 times. In Canada, between 2000 and 2015, the population of Ghanaian migrants grew 1.6-fold.

Figure 2.4. Evolution of the Ghanaian diaspora in main OECD destination countries, 2000-20

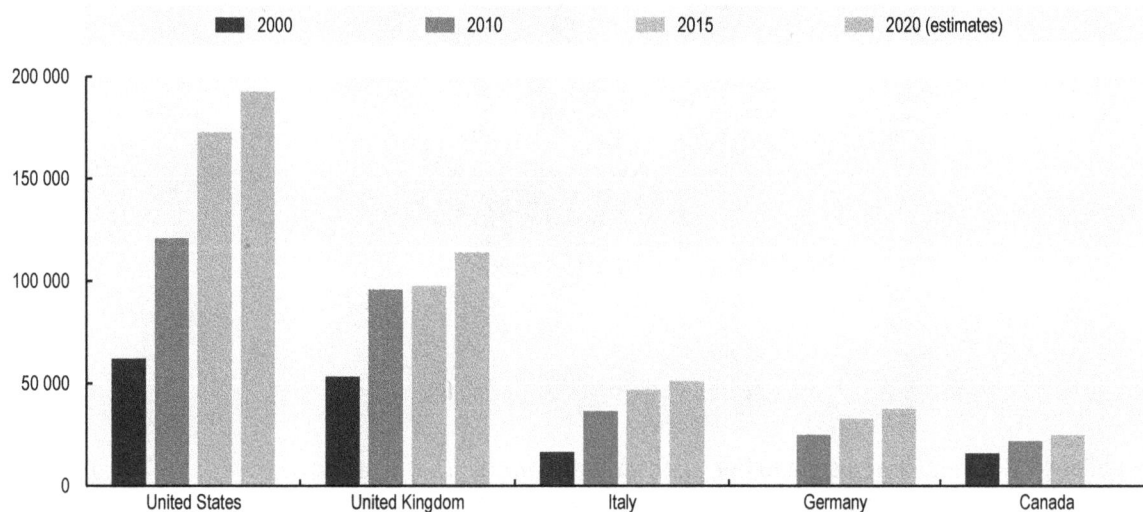

Note: Reference population includes all persons.
Source: Data for 2000, 2010 and 2015: OECD Database on Immigrants in OECD Countries (DIOC). Data for 2020: OECD Secretariat estimates.

Of the Ghanaian population residing abroad, approximately 13 800 are refugees (Box 2.3). Refugees are, theoretically, estimated as part of the foreign-born population in their respective host countries, but in practice, this depends on data sources and host country practices.

Box 2.3. Ghanaian refugees and asylum seekers

In 2020, there were approximately 14 000 Ghanaian refugees worldwide. The refugee population is highly concentrated in neighbouring Togo, which hosts 61% of the total (Figure 2.5). Between 1982 and 1994 and, subsequently, between 2010 and 2014, land disputes and inter-ethnic clashes caused thousands of Ghanaians to flee to rural communities in northern Togo, where they have strong cultural and linguistic affinities with the local population (UNHCR, 2018[4])

In 2020, the second largest country of asylum was Italy, with 18% of Ghanaian refugees (approximately 2 500), and Germany, which hosted an additional 5% (600). However, while the number of refugees has remained relatively stable since 1994 (between 14 000 and 18 000), the number of asylum seekers from Ghana grew 10-fold between 2000 and 2020. As of 2020, there were approximately 10 000 Ghanaian pending asylum applications worldwide. More significantly, Ghanaian individuals seek

---

asylum in a wider variety of countries, with increasing numbers turning to Latin America. In 2020, Brazil was the top destination country for Ghanaian asylum seekers with approximately 2 500 (24% of the total), a trend that gained notoriety in the 2014 World Cup when the Brazilian Government processed 1 000 asylum applications from Ghanaian individuals, a 6-fold increase from the previous year.

Figure 2.5. Distribution of Ghanaian refugees in main destination countries, 2020

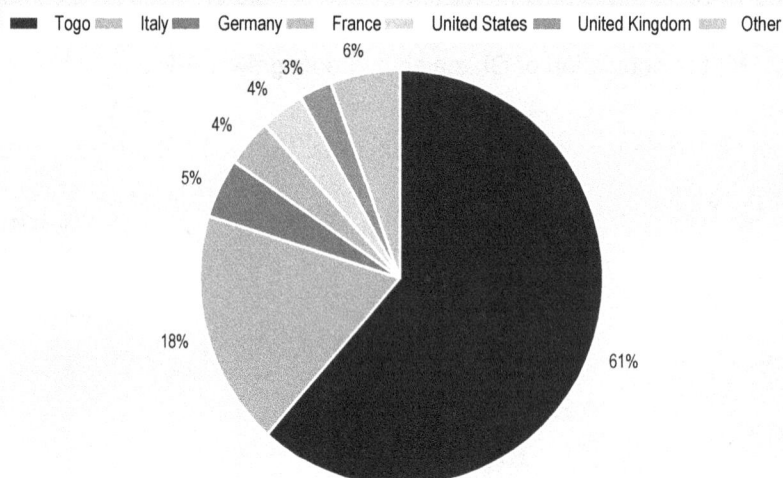

Legend: Togo, Italy, Germany, France, United States, United Kingdom, Other

- Togo: 61%
- Italy: 18%
- Germany: 5%
- France: 4%
- United States: 4%
- United Kingdom: 3%
- Other: 6%

Source: UNHCR, 2020.

International students comprise another specific category of Ghanaian emigrants. In 2019, more than 9 000 students from Ghana were enrolled in a tertiary-level institution abroad, representing roughly 2% of all tertiary-level enrollments in Ghana. Nine in ten were studying in an OECD country (Figure 2.6). The total number of international students from Ghana increased by 21% in six years, from about 7 800 in 2013 to 9 400 in 2019. Among the 15 ECOWAS countries, Ghana is the fourth-largest origin country of international students in the OECD area, after Nigeria, Senegal and Côte d'Ivoire.

Across OECD countries, the United States hosted the largest number of students from Ghana in 2019, accounting for 37% of the total. Two other English-speaking countries, the United Kingdom and Canada, are also significant destinations for Ghanaian students (1 800 and 1 000, respectively). However, while the number of Ghanaian students slightly decreased in the United Kingdom between 2013 and 2019 (-8%), it almost doubled in Canada during the same period (+87%). Among the top five destinations for Ghanaian international students, Germany registered the largest percentage increase in recent years: from approximately 300 in 2013, it hosted 1 000 students in 2019, a 3-fold increase.

Figure 2.6. Main destination countries for international students from Ghana, 2013 and 2019

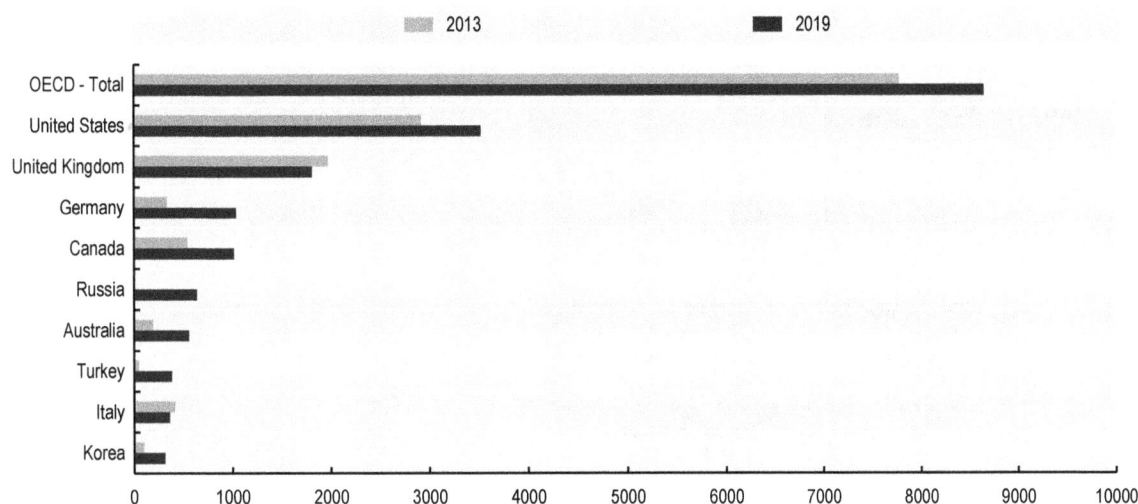

Notes: Enrolled Ghanaian students (who are not citizens of the destination country) in a tertiary education programme.
Source: OECD/Eurostat/UNESCO Institute for Statistics (2021), *Education at a Glance Database*.

Regional distribution of Ghanaian emigrants in selected destination countries

National data sources make it possible to study the location of Ghanaian emigrants in the three main destination countries and map their regional distribution. In the United States, Ghanaian migrants have settled across the country, but New York accounts for the largest concentration, hosting one in five Ghanaian migrants, followed by the states of Virginia and New Jersey. This geographic concentration is not exclusive to Ghanaian migrants, as most African migrants, more generally, reside in these three states (United States Census Bureau, 2019[5]). As compared to the foreign and native-born population of the United States, the Ghanaian diaspora is overrepresented in the Northeast region (home to the states of New York and New Jersey), which hosts 40% of the total (Figure 2.7).

In the second-largest country of destination, the United Kingdom, Ghanaian emigrants are mostly located in London (67% of the total), where they are overrepresented compared to the foreign-born (40%) and other migrants from West Africa (61%). Job opportunities in the local economy, in the informal sector, in particular, have been an important pull factor for Ghanaian migrants, coupled with strong social networks that have developed around certain boroughs (Southwark, Lambeth, Newham, Hackney, Haringey, Lewisham, Croydon and Brent) (Vasta, 2010[6]). The second-largest regional concentration is located in South East England, which hosts 10% of Ghanaian migrants, followed by East England, accounting for 7% of the total (Figure 2.8).

In Italy, most Ghanaian migrants live in the northern regions (Figure 2.9). Legislative measures that offered a pathway to legalisation and better employment opportunities drove Ghanaian migrants to northern Italy, even when they first settled in the southern regions. Emilia Romagna hosts the largest concentration of Ghanaian migrants (23% of the total) due to a combination of job opportunities in highly specialised small and medium-sized enterprises of the industrial and manufacturing sectors and a favourable legislative environment (Marabello, 2018[7]). For instance, only Emilia Romagna and Tuscany have modified their regional statuses to allow migrants to participate in local administrative elections.

Figure 2.7. Regional distribution of Ghanaian emigrants in the United States, 2017-19

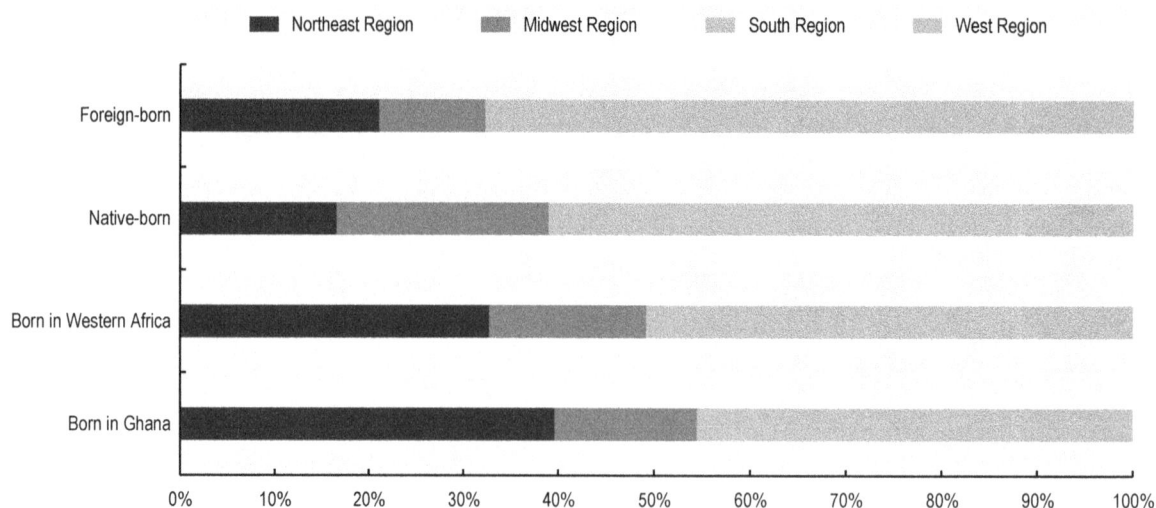

Note: Western Africa in ACS comprises Benin, Burkina Faso, Cabo Verde, Cote d'Ivoire, The Gambia, Ghana, Guinea, Guinea-Bissau, Liberia, Mali, Mauritania, Niger, Nigeria, St. Helena, Senegal, Sierra Leone, and Togo. Compared to the ECOWAS group, this category includes two additional countries: St. Helena and Mauritania.
Source: American Community Survey 1-Year Estimates; pooled data from 2017, 2018, 2019.

Figure 2.8. Regional distribution of Ghanaian emigrants in the United Kingdom, 2011

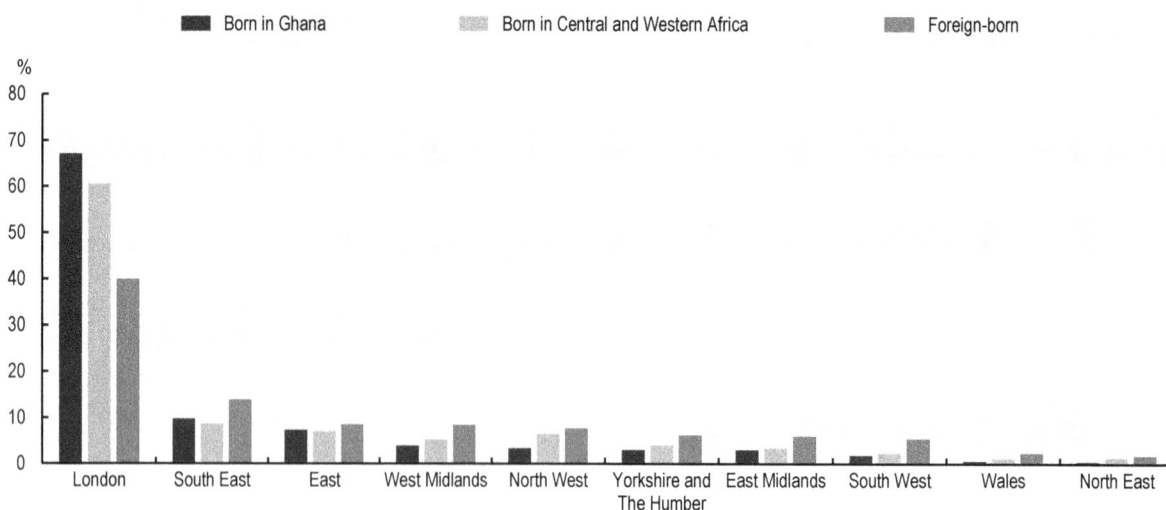

Note: Central and Western Africa in the UK Census comprise Ghana, Nigeria and "Other" countries.
Source: United Kingdom Census 2011.

Figure 2.9. Regional distribution of Ghanaian emigrants in Italy, 2020

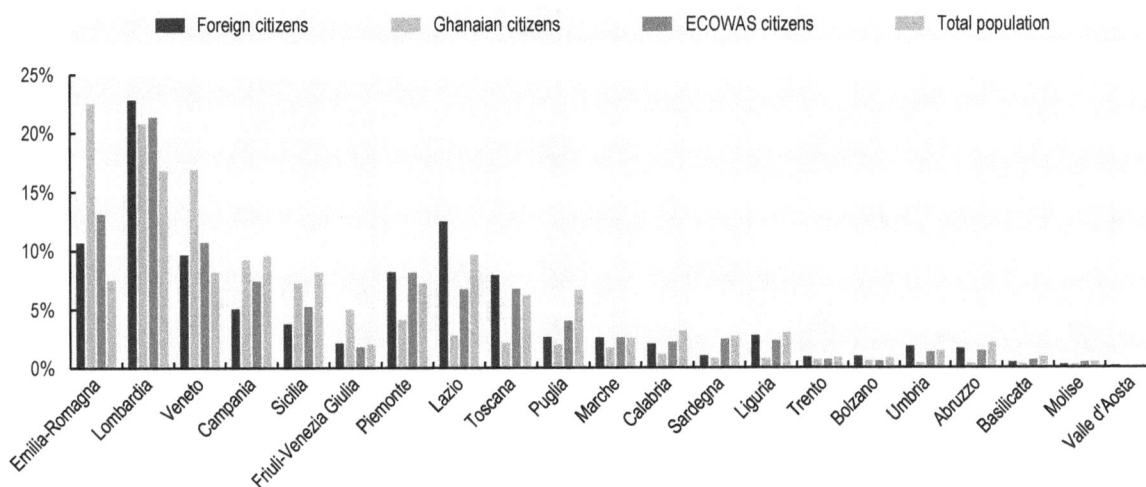

Note: The foreign population is determined by country of citizenship in Italian census data.
Source: Istat, 2020.

The demographic composition of the Ghanaian diaspora

Women comprise 47% of the Ghanaian diaspora in OECD countries

In 2015/16, 47% of Ghanaian migrants living in OECD countries were women. The Ghanaian diaspora shows a very similar composition to the average emigrant population from ECOWAS countries (46% of which is composed of women). Its share of women is only slightly inferior to the foreign-born population's (51%). Ghana's is the sixth most feminised diaspora among ECOWAS countries after Cabo Verde, Liberia, Sierra Leone, Côte d'Ivoire and Nigeria (Figure 2.10).

Although certain studies point to an increasing feminisation of the Ghanaian emigrant population – with women moving independently as skilled workers, entrepreneurs and traders – the gender composition of the Ghanaian diaspora in OECD countries has remained practically stable for 15 years. Between 2000/01 and 2015/16, the share of women only increased by 1 percentage point. However, there is evidence that Ghanaian women dominate short distance emigration to neighbouring countries (Anarfi, 2017[8]; UNDESA, 2020[9]). Ghana implemented structural adjustment policies in the 1980s, which increased unemployment and underemployment, incentivising women to emigrate as an alternative livelihood strategy. At the same time, economic opportunities in West Africa and the end of the apartheid in South Africa in the early 1990s propelled female migration within the continent (Wong, 2006[10]). In more recent years, women have increasingly engaged in international migration through specific sectors of occupation. The phenomenon is evident among women who emigrate as nurses and health care professionals to the United Kingdom and as domestic workers to countries in the Middle East (IOM, 2019[11]).

Figure 2.10. Share of women in the emigrant population from Ghana and ECOWAS countries living in OECD countries, 2015/16

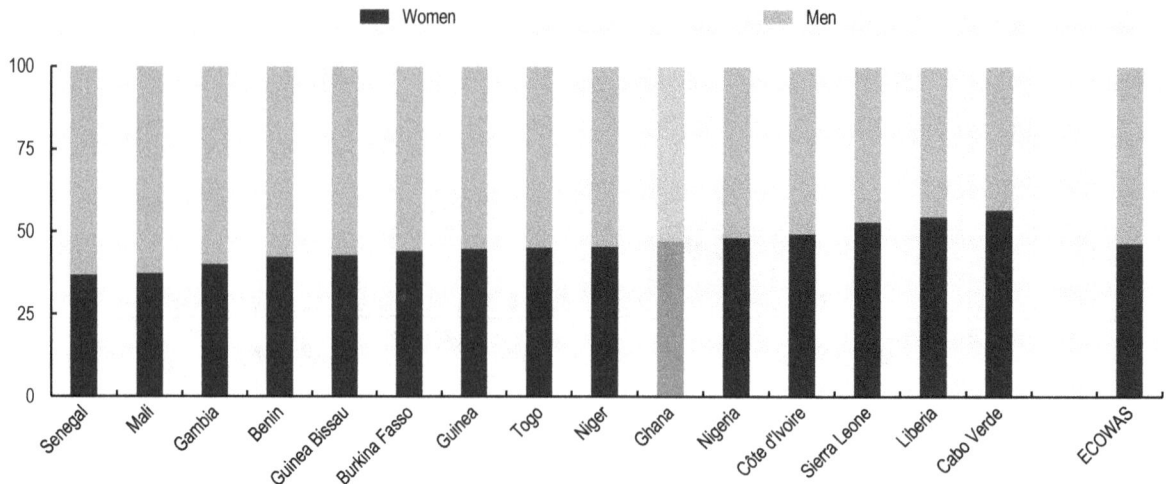

Note: Reference population includes all persons.
Source: OECD Database on Immigrants in OECD Countries (DIOC), 2015/16.

The distribution of women in the Ghanaian diaspora varies significantly by country of destination (Figure 2.12). Women represent 55% of the Ghanaian diaspora in the United Kingdom, the only leading destination country where women outnumber men. However, the phenomenon is not limited to the Ghanaian diaspora as women also represent the majority of the African diaspora in the United Kingdom (OECD/AFD, 2019[12]). In Italy, by contrast, Ghanaian women only account for 37% of the total emigrant population. Evidence suggests that it was not until the mid-1990s that married women and children began migrating to Italy (Marabello, 2018[7]). In the United States, Germany and Canada, the gender ratio is more balanced (47% of women in the United States and 49% in the latter two countries).

Eight in ten Ghanaian migrants living in OECD countries are of working age

The Ghanaian diaspora living in OECD countries is primarily of working age: 80% of its emigrants were between 25 and 64 years old in 2015/16, similar to that of ECOWAS emigrants, 77% of which belong to the same age group (Figure 2.11). The predominance of working-age individuals in the Ghanaian diaspora is more significant than among the foreign-born and native populations of OECD countries (+11% and +29%, respectively). This positive self-selection among Ghanaian individuals of working age also means that the share of Ghanaian emigrants younger than 15 and above 64 is disproportionately low.

The population younger than 15 accounts for 5% of the Ghanaian diaspora in OECD countries, a similar share than among the foreign-born population (6%) but significantly lower than among the native-born (19%). Similarly, individuals older than 64 represent 6% of the Ghanaian diaspora, compared to 17 and 15% of native and foreign-born populations, respectively.

Moreover, the age distribution of the Ghanaian emigrant population highly contrasts with the population of Ghana and, again, points to positive self-selection among those in conditions to work: only four out of ten Ghanaians are of working age, compared to eight out of ten emigrants. Similarly, 38% of the Ghanaian population is less than 15 years old, compared to 5% of the population that migrates to an OECD country.

However, the age distribution of the Ghanaian diaspora varies significantly by country of destination (Figure 2.12). The Ghanaian migrant population in the United Kingdom is older than in the rest of the main destination countries: the share of individuals over 64 years of age is 8%, compared to 6% in the

United States and Canada and 3% in Germany. In Italy, due to the low number of observations captured in Labour Force Surveys, data suggest that the population of Ghanaian migrants older than 64 is virtually non-existent. Aside from the methodological limitations of survey samples, it must be noted that substantial emigration to the Anglophone countries preceded emigration to Southern Europe, and Italy in particular. Further, surveys among Ghanaian migrants in Italy suggest that most plan to return before pension age and invest in Ghana to support such plans (Akwasi, 2016[13])

Italy and Germany host the largest proportions of Ghanaian migrants of working age (85% of the total migrant population in both countries). Conversely, the United States hosts the largest proportion of children: the share of people less than 15 years old is 8% compared to 3% in the United Kingdom, reflecting the preponderance of permanent family emigration to the United States.

Two countries stand out from the point of view of gender and age distribution: on the one hand, in Italy, 58% of men are of working age, compared to 31% of women, the most significant gender disparity observed in the main destination countries. Conversely, in the United Kingdom, we observe a larger proportion of women of working age (46%) than men (33%).

Figure 2.11. Distribution of Ghanaian emigrants in OECD countries by age groups, 2015/16

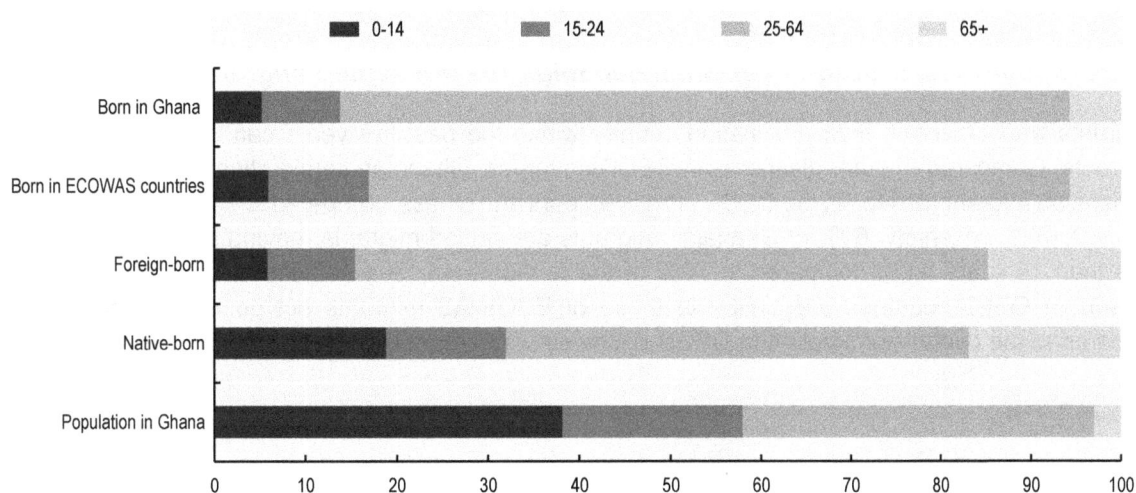

Note: Born in Ghana: individuals born in Ghana living in OECD countries in 2015/16. Born in ECOWAS countries: individuals born in an ECOWAS country living in OECD countries in 2015/16. Foreign-born: all immigrants living in OECD countries in 2015/16. Native-born: individuals born in an OECD country and living in their country of birth in 2015/16. Population in Ghana: individuals living in Ghana in 2015/16.
Source: OECD Database on Immigrants in OECD Countries (DIOC), 2015/16; Population in Ghana: UNDESA World Population Prospects (2015 estimates).

Figure 2.12. Distribution of Ghanaian emigrants in selected OECD countries by age and sex, 2015/16

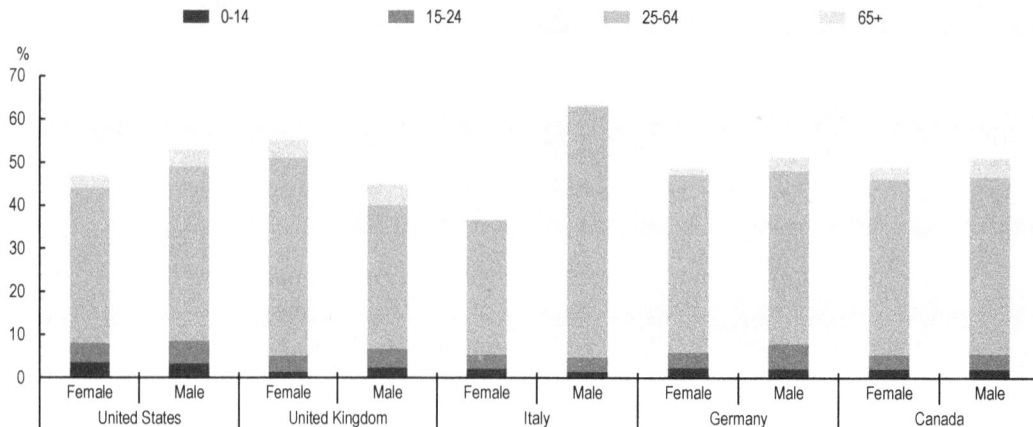

Source: OECD Database on Immigrants in OECD Countries (DIOC), 2015/16.

In OECD countries, six out of ten Ghanaian migrants are settled migrants

Emigrants who arrived in their destination country within the past five years can be considered recent emigrants. Compared to other diasporas in OECD countries, Ghanaian immigration is more recent: 22% of Ghanaian migrants arrived in the OECD area five years ago or less, compared to 16% of the foreign-born (Figure 2.13). Conversely, 60% of Ghanaian migrants are settled migrants (having arrived in the country more than 10 years ago), compared to 70% of the foreign-born. The settlement patterns of Ghanaian migrants in OECD countries are similar to those of ECOWAS migrants but point to relative recency compared to the overall immigration to OECD countries.

Figure 2.13.Distribution of Ghanaian emigrants in OECD countries by duration of stay, 2015/16

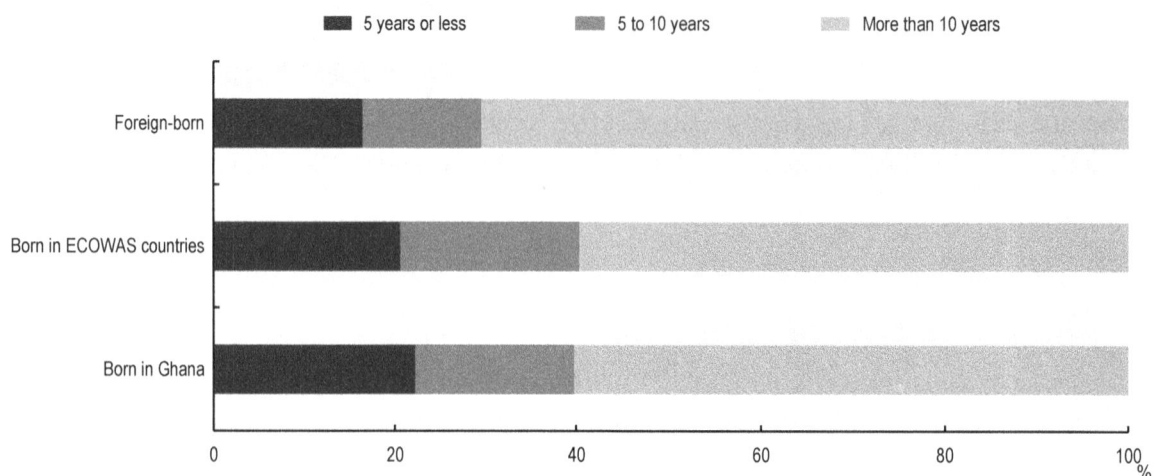

Note: Population 15 years and older.
Source: OECD Database on Immigrants in OECD Countries (DIOC), 2015/16.

Differences in the distribution of the length of stay of Ghanaian emigrants by destination country make it possible to identify the different migration dynamics at work in OECD countries (Figure 2.14). Among the main destination countries, Canada and the United Kingdom are the host countries with the highest average length of stay: 78 and 68% of Ghanaian migrants, respectively, stayed for more than ten years. In contrast, a third of the Ghanaian migrants in Germany stayed in the country for five years or less. Similarly, more than half (55%) of Ghanaian migrants stayed in Italy for no more than ten years. These trends point to longer-term settlement prospects in the Anglophone countries and more temporary emigration to Italy and Germany.

Figure 2.14. Distribution of Ghanaian emigrants by duration of stay in main OECD destination countries, 2015/16

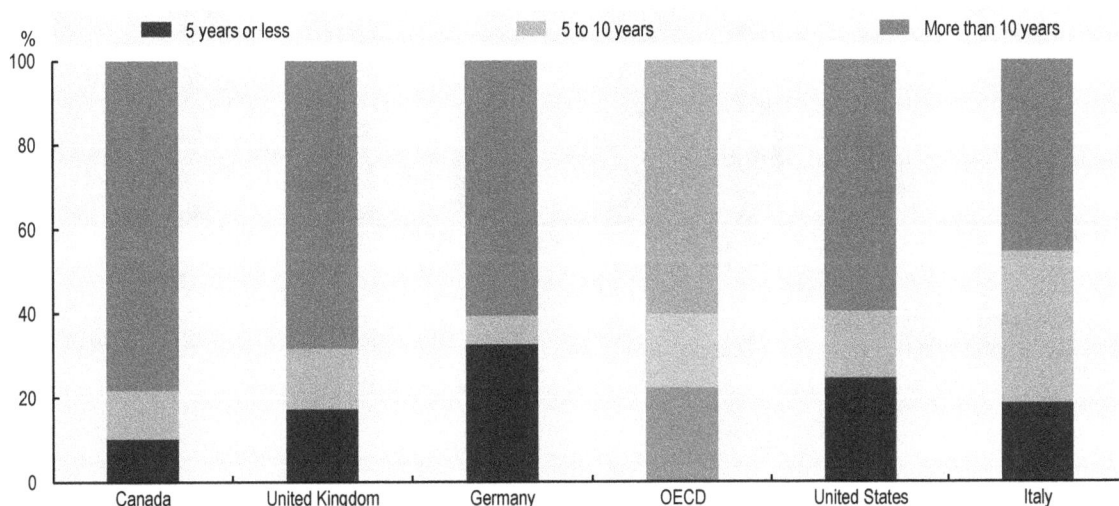

Note: Population 15 years and older.
Source: OECD Database on Immigrants in OECD Countries (DIOC), 2015/16.

Education distribution among Ghanaian emigrants across OECD countries

In 2015/16, more than a third of Ghanaian emigrants aged 15 years and older were tertiary-educated

In 2015/16, more than a third (35%) of Ghanaian migrants aged 15 years and older and living in OECD countries had a tertiary education (Figure 2.15). The share of highly educated migrants from Ghana is almost on par with the ECOWAS average (37%) and slightly higher than the foreign-born average (33%).

While the share of low educated migrants from Ghana has remained practically unchanged between 2000 and 2015, the share of medium and highly educated emigrants has evolved in contrary directions, albeit at low rates: in 2015/16, 37% of emigrants had medium educational attainment, a 3% decrease since 2000. Conversely, the share of emigrants with high educational attainment grew by 2% during the same period.

Ghanaian emigrants to OECD countries also hold significantly higher educational credentials than the average Ghanaian population, reflecting a strong positive selection of migrants from developing countries to the OECD area. Further, the share of the Ghanaian population with high educational attainment remained practically stable between 2000 and 2015, increasing only 1 percentage point during this period. Conversely, among the emigrant population, the share of highly educated increased by 2 percentage points, which suggests a widening gap between the origin and emigrant population. Regarding the

ECOWAS population, Ghana ranks in the middle in educational attainment: six countries have higher shares of highly educated emigrants, and eight rank below (Figure 2.16).

Figure 2.15. Educational attainment among Ghanaian emigrants in OECD countries, 2000/01 and 2015/16

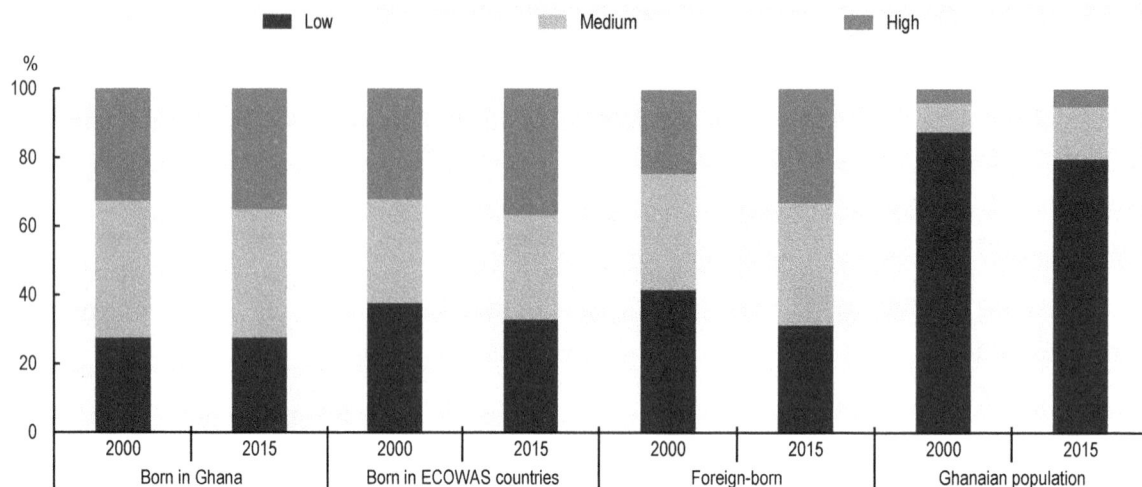

Note: Population 15 years and older.
Source: OECD Database on Immigrants in OECD Countries (DIOC), 2015/16; Wittgenstein Centre for Demography and Global Human Capital (2018).

Figure 2.16. Educational attainment among emigrants from Ghana and ECOWAS countries living in OECD countries, 2015/16

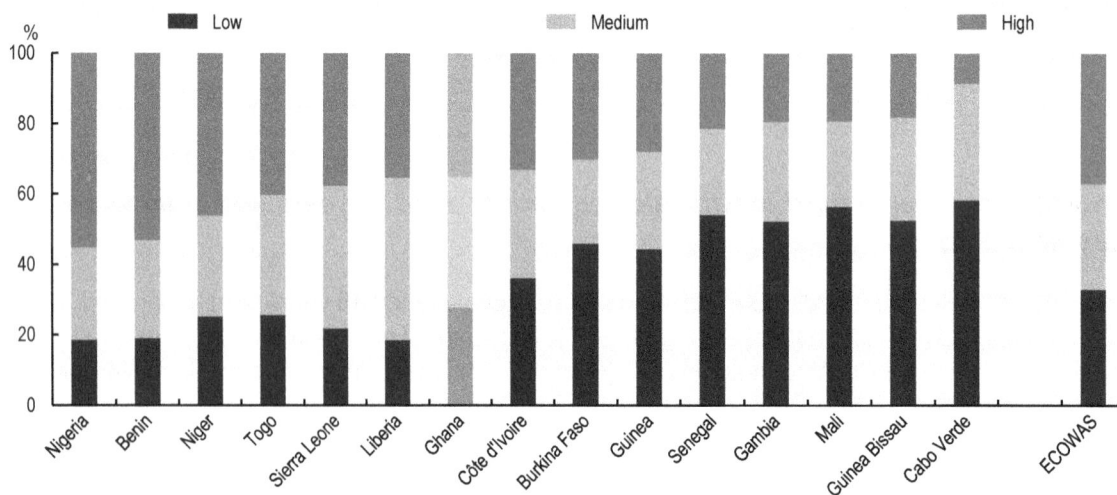

Note: Population 15 years and older.
Source: OECD Database on Immigrants in OECD Countries (DIOC), 2015/16.

Ghanaian emigrants with a high level of education mostly settle in English-speaking countries

Overall, in 2015/16, 35% of Ghanaian migrants aged 15 and older living in OECD countries had tertiary education. There is, however, heterogeneity across destination countries (Figure 2.17). In the top OECD destination country, the United States, almost half of the Ghanaian migrants (45%) have a high level of education. While the United States does not host the largest share of tertiary-educated migrants from Ghana (surpassed by Canada, with 66%), it does present the lowest share of low educated. To a lesser extent, Ghanaian migrants in the United Kingdom – the country with the second largest diaspora – also have high levels of education: the share of tertiary-educated among them is 41%, but the share of low educated is higher than in the United States, at 26%. These two profiles contrast with the third and fourth most important destination countries: in Italy and Germany, most Ghanaian migrants (69 and 51%, respectively) are low educated and only a minority have a tertiary education (4 and 9%, respectively). These differences confirm that highly educated Ghanaians tend to migrate to English-speaking destinations to be able to practice their professions, with a higher representation of lower-educated migrants in countries such as Germany, Italy and the Netherlands (Schans, 2013[14])

Figure 2.17. Educational attainment among Ghanaian emigrants in main OECD destination countries, 2015/16

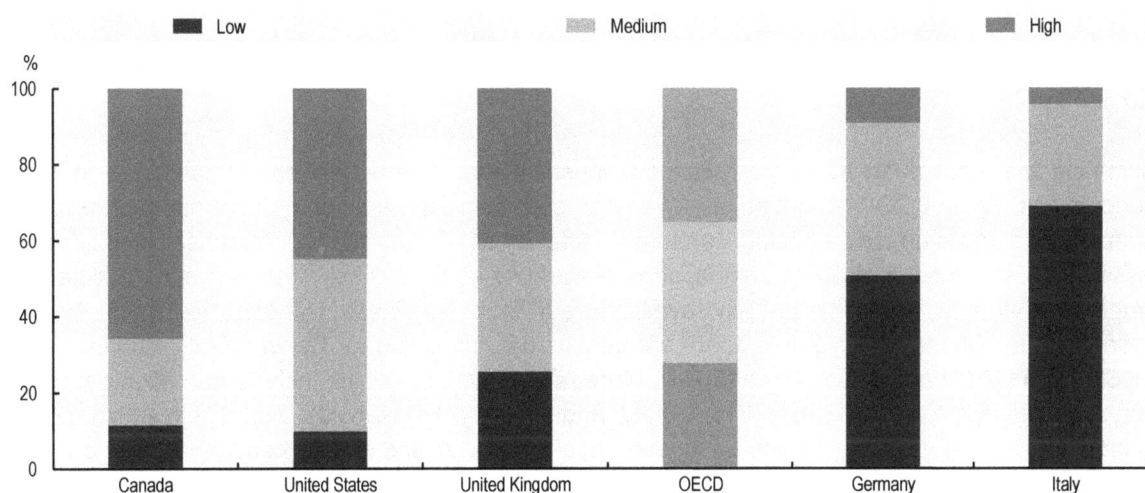

Note: Population 15 years and older.
Source: OECD Database on Immigrants in OECD Countries (DIOC), 2015/16.

Ghanaian emigrant women have, on average, a lower educational level than men but the gap between them has narrowed since 2000

In 2015/16, Ghanaian emigrant women to OECD countries had, on average, a lower educational level than their male counterparts, but the gap between them has narrowed significantly since 2000 (Figure 2.18). While the educational attainment of Ghanaian emigrant women improved overall, it decreased for men between 2000 and 2015. For instance, in 2015/16 one-third of women had tertiary education, 7 percentage points higher than in 2000. Conversely, the share of men with a tertiary education decreased by 1 percentage point in the same period. Further, while the share of low-educated women decreased by 5 percentage points during the same period, it increased by 4 percentage points among men.

Figure 2.18. Level of education among Ghanaian emigrants by sex in OECD countries, 2000/01 and 2015/16

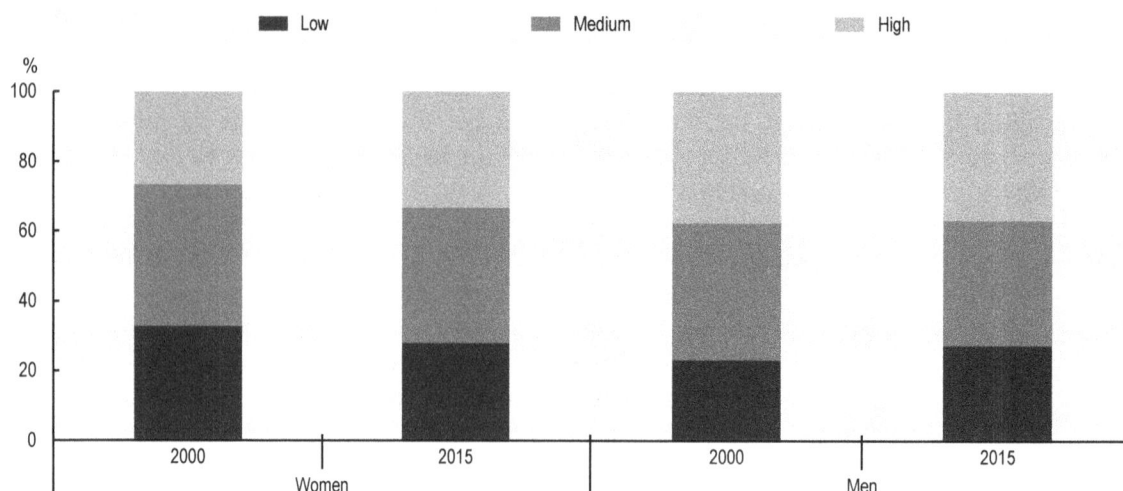

Note: Population 15 years and older.
Source: OECD Database on Immigrants in OECD Countries (DIOC), 2000/01 and 2015/16.

Box 2.4. The Ghanaian diaspora in African countries

Estimating the size of the Ghanaian diaspora in sub-Saharan Africa is problematic due to data shortcomings. While ECOWAS countries have been collecting statistical data on immigration through the national population and housing censuses, differences in definitions, reference periods, and classification schemes complicate comparisons (Awumbila et al., 2014[15]). Further, census data are comprehensive and generally publicly available but lack timeliness. Among the main African destinations for Ghanaian emigrants, there are census data available for Benin (2013), Burkina Faso (2006), Togo (2010) and South Africa (2011). More recent surveys, which include migration data, are also available for Côte d'Ivoire (2015 Equity and Poverty Household) and South Africa (2016 Community Survey). Nigeria, the top destination country, conducted its last census in 2006 and the foreign component is unavailable.

Albeit the limitations, it is possible to build a socio-demographic profile of the average Ghanaian migrant in sub-Saharan Africa. In terms of gender composition, women account for most migrant stocks in three of the five countries for which data are available (Benin, Burkina Faso and Togo) (Figure 2.19). Women represent approximately two-thirds of the Ghanaian emigrant population in neighbouring Togo and Burkina Faso.

As in OECD countries, most of the Ghanaian migrant population in African countries is of working age (15-64), but the age distribution is more balanced, with comparative higher shares of children and elders, which points to other types of migration patterns aside from labour migration. In terms of educational distribution, over 90% of Ghanaian emigrants are low-educated (Figure 2.20). The only exception to this pattern is South Africa, which attracts a significant share of medium and high-educated migrants from Ghana (45 and 31%, respectively).

Figure 2.19. Distribution of the Ghanaian emigrant population by sex and age in selected African countries, several years

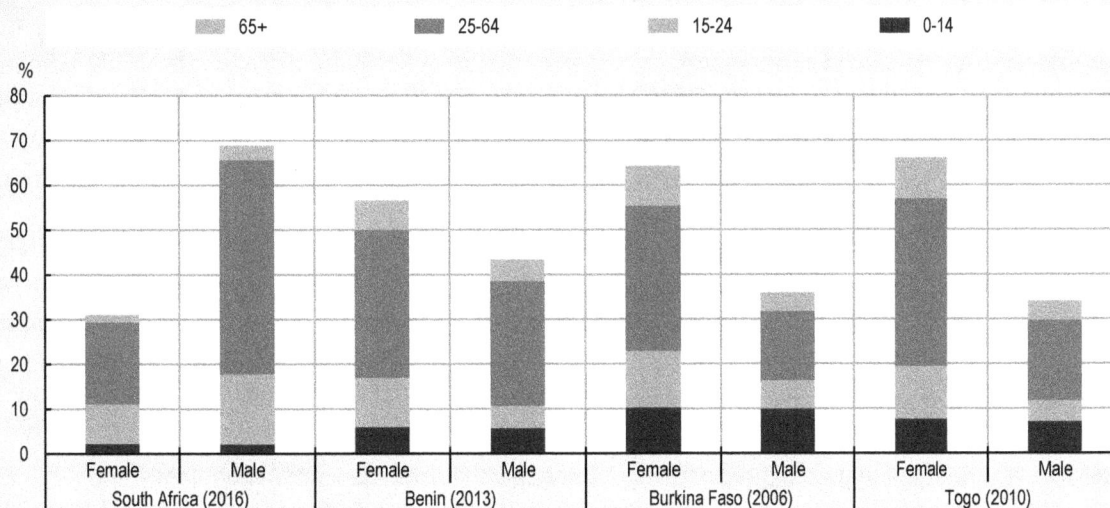

Note: Population 15 years and older. Côte d'Ivoire estimates the migrant population by nationality.
Source: Togo: 2010 General Census of the Population and Habitat via IPUMS; Burkina Faso: 2006 General Population and Housing Census via IPUMS; Benin: 2013 Population and Housing Census via IPUMS; Côte d'Ivoire; 2015 Equity and Poverty Household; South Africa: 2016 Community Survey via IPUMS.

Figure 2.20. Educational distribution of Ghanaian emigrants by sex in selected African countries, several years

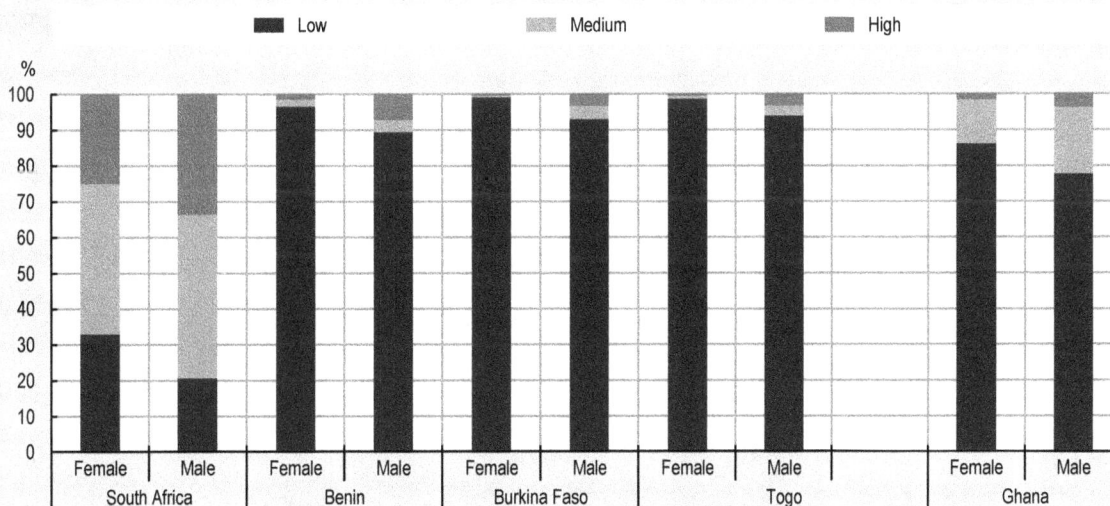

Note: Reference population includes persons aged 15 and over. In Côte d'Ivoire, the migrant population is estimated by nationality.
Source: Togo: 2010 General Census of the Population and Habitat via IPUMS; Burkina Faso: 2006 General Population and Housing Census via IPUMS; Benin: 2013 Population and Housing Census; Côte d'Ivoire; 2015 Equity and Poverty Household; South Africa: 2016 Community Survey via IPUMS.

Acquisition of nationality among Ghanaian emigrants in OECD countries

Access to the host-country nationality is an important element of integration policy, as it provides immigrants with the full range of rights and duties that host-country nationals enjoy (OECD, 2010[16]). Ghana recognised dual citizenship in the mid-1990s, though implementation did not materialise until 2002, with the passing of the Dual Citizenship Act (Whitaker, 2011[17]). In 1995, approximately 200 Ghanaian migrants acquired the citizenship of their OECD host country. By 2005, that number had increased by 45% to almost 10 000. Overall, the number of Ghanaian emigrants that acquired the citizenship of an OECD country increased significantly since 1995: the numbers saw a 68-fold increase by 2019, the latest data available.

Among the leading destination countries – the United States, United Kingdom, Italy, Germany and Canada – the number of Ghanaian migrants that acquired the citizenship of their host country increased by 78%, from less than 7 000 in 2000 to 12 500 in 2019 (Figure 2.21). However, there are important differences across destinations: between 2000 and 2019 the number of Ghanaian migrants that acquired the citizenship of the United States, Italy and Germany increased, but decreased in Canada and the United Kingdom during the same period.

The number of Ghanaian migrants that acquired American citizenship has grown constantly and more than tripled (+238%) between 2000 and 2019 (Figure 2.21). In 2015, the naturalisation rate of 55% among Ghanaian migrants was only 1 percentage point higher than among the foreign-born population (Figure 2.22). Conversely, the number of Ghanaian migrants acquiring British citizenship decreased by 7% between 2000 and 2019. Yet, in 2015, the naturalisation rate among Ghanaian migrants (54%) was higher than among the foreign-born population (39%). The number of Ghanaian migrants that acquired Italian citizenship saw a 7-fold increase since 2006 (the earliest data available). However, the naturalisation rate for Ghanaian migrants in 2015 was still low, at 10%, and significantly below the naturalisation rate for the foreign-born population (27%). The number of Ghanaians who acquired German citizenship increased by 13% but started at a much lower base (approximately 700). Similar to the case of Italy, the naturalisation rate among Ghanaian migrants in Germany is low (25%) and below the rate observed for the foreign-born population (40%).

Figure 2.21. Number of Ghanaian emigrants that acquired the nationality of their host country, OECD selected countries, 1995-2019

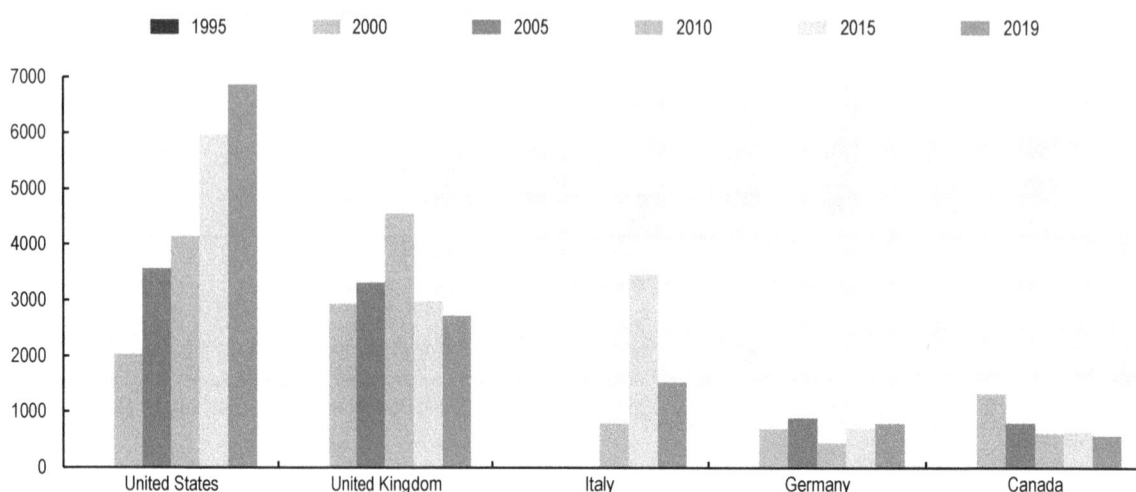

Source: OECD International Migration Database.

Figure 2.22. Rate of nationality acquisition among emigrants from Ghana living in OECD countries, 2015/16

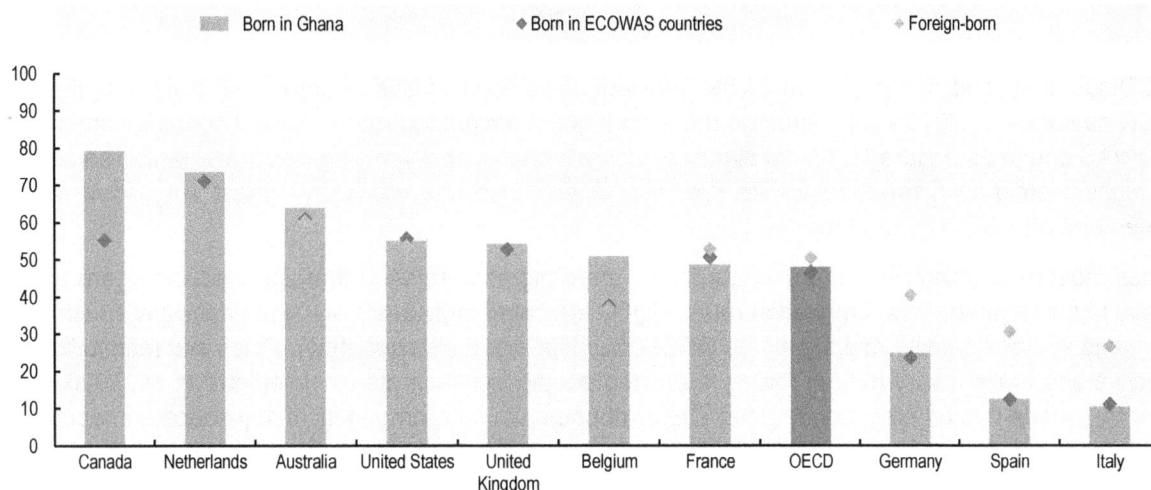

Source: OECD Database on Immigrants in OECD Countries (DIOC), 2015/16.

48% of Ghanaian emigrants held the citizenship of their OECD host country in 2015/16

According to the most recent data available, 48% of Ghanaian emigrants held the citizenship of their OECD host country (Figure 2.24). This figure is only 1 percentage point higher than for ECOWAS emigrants and 3 percentage points lower than the foreign-born population in OECD countries. Among the ECOWAS group, Ghana is the sixth country with the highest rate of naturalisations.

Figure 2.23. Rate of nationality acquisition among emigrants from the ECOWAS area living in OECD countries, 2015/16

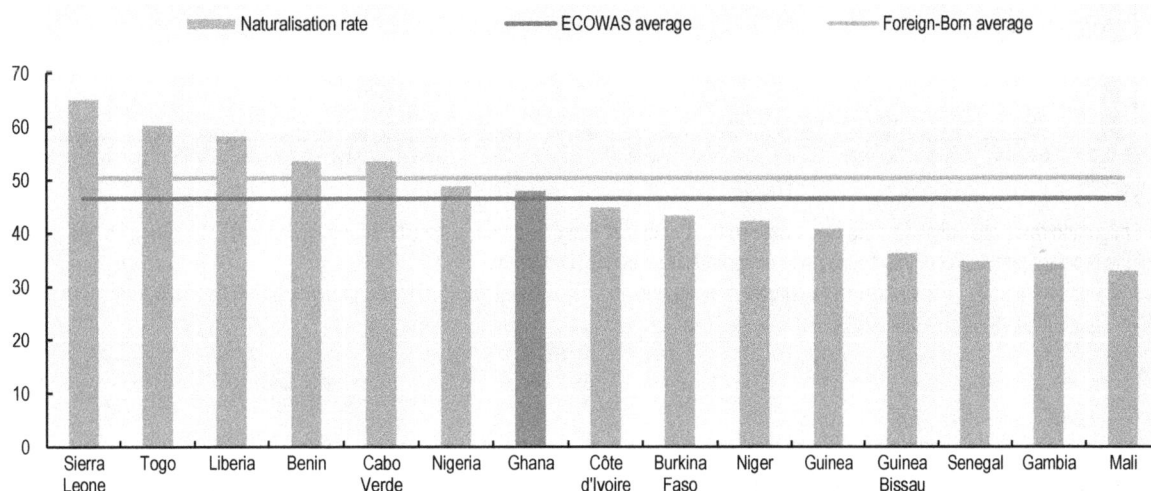

Note: Percentage of ECOWAS migrants holding the citizenship of the OECD country where they reside. The reference population includes all persons.
Source: OECD Database on Immigrants in OECD Countries (DIOC), 2015/16.

Emigration rate

Ghana has the sixth-highest emigration rate among ECOWAS countries

Emigration rates are defined as the ratio between the number of emigrants from a specific country living in OECD countries and the total sum of the resident population of this country and emigrants living in OECD countries. In 2015/16, Ghana had the sixth-highest emigration rate to OECD countries among the ECOWAS countries (Figure 2.24), but significantly lower than Cape Verde, for example, which has one of the highest emigration rates worldwide (26.1%). Ghana also has the sixth-highest emigration rate of women among ECOWAS countries (2.1%).

Across most developing and emerging countries, the emigration rates of the highly educated are almost always higher than the total emigration rates. Highly educated individuals are less financially constrained to engage in cross-country migration, and OECD countries have also adopted policies that tend to be very selective and make it very difficult for low-educated people to immigrate (d'Aiglepierre et al., 2020[18]). In 2015/16, Ghana had an emigration rate to OECD countries of 14% among its highly educated population, the seventh-highest among the 15 ECOWAS countries. The overall emigration rate of highly educated individuals to OECD countries was 16% in the same year (d'Aiglepierre et al., 2020[18]).

Figure 2.24. Emigration rates of ECOWAS countries to OECD countries, 2015/16

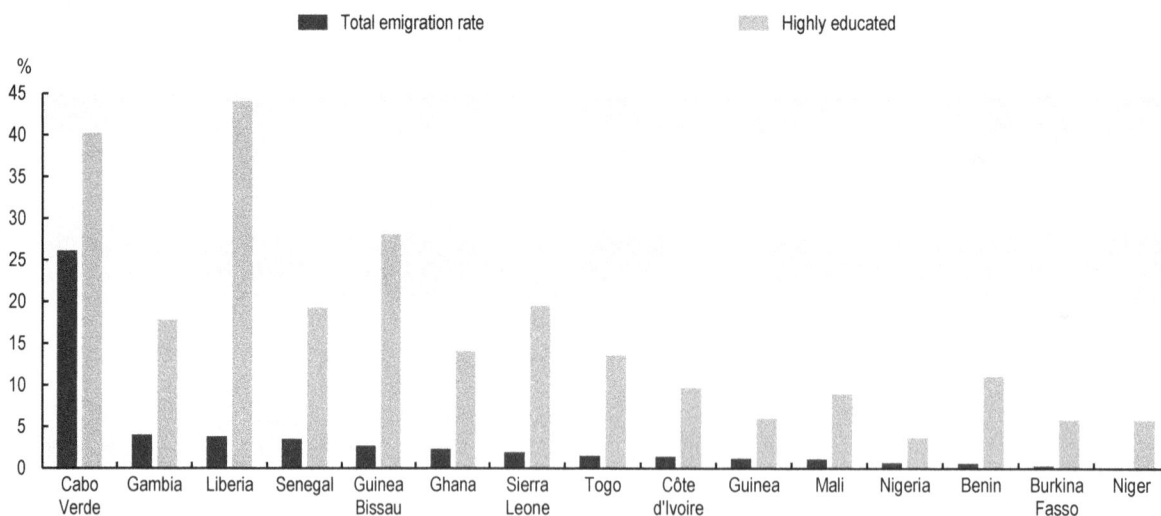

Note: Emigration rates are defined as the ratio between the number of emigrants from a specific country living in OECD countries and the total sum of the resident population of this country and emigrants living in OECD countries.
Source: d'Aiglepierre et al. (2020[18]), "A global profile of emigrants to OECD countries: Younger and more skilled migrants from more diverse countries", https://doi.org/10.1787/0cb305d3-en.

Conclusion

This chapter analysed the number of Ghanaian emigrants in main OECD destination countries, and the overall evolution of the emigrant population since 2000. Approximately half of the Ghanaian diaspora resides in the OECD area and is highly concentrated in five countries, of which two are Anglophone countries. While the stocks in OECD countries are mainly composed of men, available census data suggest that women compose most of the stocks in neighbouring countries. The educational level ad age distribution of the Ghanaian emigrant population in the OECD area shows positive self-selection among the tertiary-educated and those of working age.

References

Akwasi, E. (2016), "Connecting Return Intentions and Home Investment: the case of Ghanaian Migrants in Southern Europe", *Journal of International Migration and Integration*, Vol. 17, pp. 745-759, https://doi.org/10.1007/s12134-015-0432-2. [13]

Anarfi, J. (2017), *A Historical Perspective of Migration from and to Ghana*, University of Ghana. [8]

Awumbila, M. et al. (2014), *Across Artificial Borders: An Assessment of labour migration in the ECOWAS region*. [15]

d'Aiglepierre, R. et al. (2020), "A global profile of emigrants to OECD countries: Younger and more skilled migrants from more diverse countries", *OECD Social, Employment and Migration Working Papers*, No. 239, OECD Publishing, Paris, https://doi.org/10.1787/0cb305d3-en. [18]

IOM (2020), *Migration in Ghana. A Country Profile 2019*. [1]

IOM (2019), *Ghanaian Domestic Workers in the Middle East*. [11]

Koyi Teye, J., D. Badasu and C. Yeboah (2017), *Assessment of remittances-related services and practices of financial institutions in Ghana*. [2]

Marabello, S. (2018), "West African Migrations to Italy: An Anthropological Analysis of Ghanaian and Senegalese Politics of Mobility in Emilia Romagna", *Revue européenne des migrations internationales*, Vol. 34/1, pp. 127-149, https://doi.org/10.4000/remi.10193. [7]

OECD (2016), *Perspectives on Global Development 2017: International Migration in a Shifting World*, OECD Publishing, Paris, https://doi.org/10.1787/persp_glob_dev-2017-en. [3]

OECD (2010), *International Migration Outlook 2010*, OECD Publishing, Paris, https://doi.org/10.1787/migr_outlook-2010-en. [16]

OECD/AFD (2019), "Are the characteristics and scope of African migration outside of the continent changing?", *Migration Data Brief No. 5*, OECD, Paris, https://www.oecd.org/migration/mig/Migration-data-brief-5-EN.pdf. [12]

Schans, D. (2013), *Changing Patterns of Ghanaian Migration*. [14]

UNDESA (2020), *Population DIvision: International Migration Stock*. [9]

UNHCR (2018), *Solutions in West Africa. Ghanaian Refugees*. [4]

United States Census Bureau (2019), *American Community Survey 1-Year-Estimates-Public Use MIcrodata Sample*. [5]

Vasta, E. (2010), "'London the Leveller': Ghanaian Work Strategies and Community Solidarity", *Journal of Ethnic and Migration Studies*, Vol. 36/4, pp. 581-598, https://doi.org/10.1080/13691830903398888. [6]

Whitaker, B. (2011), "The Politics of Home: Dual Citizenship and the African Diaspora", *International Migration Review*, Vol. 45/4, pp. 755-783, https://doi.org/10.1111/j.1747-7379.2011.00867.x. [17]

Wong, M. (2006), "The Gendered Politics of Remittances in Ghanaian Transnational Families", *Economic Geography*, Vol. 82/4, pp. 355-381. [10]

3 Labour market outcomes of Ghanaian emigrants

This chapter analyses Ghanaian emigrants' insertion in the labour market of destination countries, with a particular focus on the OECD area. It presents the 2015/16 employment status of emigrants aged between 15 and 64 years, with more recent data available for the United States (2017/2019) and Italy (2017/2020), the first and third destination countries in the OECD area. The chapter also analyses the dynamics of their insertion since the 2008 global recession and the 2010 Eurozone debt crisis. It provides an assessment of employment through the variables of sex, education, duration of stay and nationality. Finally, the chapter provides data on over-qualification rates, occupations and employment sectors.

In Brief

Key findings

- In 2015/16, 78% of working-age Ghanaian emigrants participated in OECD labour markets. Within the active population, 10% were unemployed. Overall, Ghanaian emigrants' insertion in OECD labour markets is comparatively better than other ECOWAS migrants.

- Seven in ten Ghanaian emigrants were employed in OECD countries, a rate 5 percentage points higher than the native-born population. The employment situation varies across destination countries, with the highest rates observed in English-speaking countries. In the United States, top destination in the OECD area, almost four Ghanaian migrants out of five were employed in 2017/19.

- Employment-wise, Ghana-born women fare better than the average female migrant in the OECD area, but Ghanaian women still present lower employment rates than their male counterparts. In 2015/16, men's employment rate, at 65%, was 11 percentage points higher than for women.

- Across OECD countries, the participation of Ghanaian migrants in the labour market increases with their level of education: 82% of those with a tertiary education were employed, compared to 54% of those with low education, with substantial variation across destination countries.

- However, higher employment rates among the tertiary educated hide a significant inadequacy between Ghanaian migrants' qualifications and their occupations in OECD countries. In the United States, over-qualification rates drop with increased time of settlement, when they have attended a tertiary education institution in the country and when they hold American citizenship.

- Substantial over-qualification rates reflect a high concentration in low-skilled occupations: a third of Ghanaian migrants held an elementary occupation in 2015/16, with substantial heterogeneity across destination countries.

- A particular feature of the labour market integration among Ghanaian emigrants is their high participation in health-related occupations, particularly in English-speaking countries. In 2015/16, 5 800 Ghanaian migrants worked as health professionals in the United Kingdom, 9% of the total Ghana-born population of working age. In the United States, 29% of the Ghana-born labour force was also employed in a health-related occupation (2017/2019).

In the OECD area, Ghanaian migrants fare better in the labour market of English-speaking countries

In 2015/16, approximately 384 000 Ghanaian migrants of working age (between 15 and 64 years old) were living in OECD countries. More than three-quarters (78%) participated in the labour market. This participation rate was 5 and 4 percentage points higher than among the foreign and native-born populations of OECD countries. While Ghanaian migrants participate in the labour market at almost equal rates to other ECOWAS migrants, they evidence higher employment rates (70 and 65%, respectively). They also present lower unemployment rates (10% for Ghana-born emigrants, compared to 15% for the average emigrant from ECOWAS countries), which point to a better insertion in the labour market of Ghanaian emigrants.

As shown in Figure 3.1, labour market participation varies significantly across the main destination countries. Higher employment rates are observed in English-speaking countries, reflecting consolidated corridors in the case of the United Kingdom and the United States, and the importance of language as a critical element in labour market integration. In the United States and the United Kingdom, employment rates among Ghanaian migrants were also higher than among the native-born in 2015/16 (+9 and +5 percentage points in the United States and the United Kingdom, respectively). More recent data from the United States confirms the tendency: in 2017/19, Ghanaian migrants' employment rates were 6 and 9 percentage points higher than among the foreign and native-born populations, respectively.

Conversely, in Germany and Italy, employment rates are much lower (54 and 53%, respectively). Ghanaian migration to Germany displays three main patterns: educational migration, humanitarian migration and family reunification (Morath, 2015[1]). Such patterns reflect in reasons for admission to the country. As explained in Chapter 1, Germany almost exclusively issued permits for family and humanitarian reasons to Ghanaian nationals between 2010 and 2020. The predominance of asylum seekers, family dependants and students over labour migrants may account for the low employment rates of Ghanaian emigrants in Germany.

Migration to Italy also displays patterns of humanitarian migration and family reunification, particularly after 2015 (see Chapter 1). Between 2000 and 2020, Italy hosted 19% of all asylum seekers from Ghana. According to (Marabello and Riccio, 2018[2]), while the agricultural sector of southern regions and the industrial and manufacturing sectors of the North attract Ghanaian male migrants, the majority of Ghanaian migrants have entered the country through family reunification. The fact that Ghanaian women are overrepresented in the share of recent migrants (who arrived in Italy less five years ago) reflect this pattern. The low unemployment rates among women, which are further described below, help explain Italy's overall low unemployment rates.

Compared to the average migrant to the OECD area and ECOWAS migrants, Ghanaian migrants display, on average, a better insertion in the OECD labour market, with employment rates 3 and 5 percentage points higher, respectively (Figure 3.2). However, the comparative advantage of Ghanaian migrants is only evident in English-speaking countries, with the highest differentials observed in the United Kingdom. In Germany and Italy, conversely, employment rates among Ghanaian migrants are 13 and 6 percentage points lower than for the average migrant, respectively. More minor differences are observed in comparison with the ECOWAS migrant population.

Figure 3.1. Labour market status of Ghanaian emigrants by main OECD destination country, 2015/16

Share of working-age population (share of the active population for unemployment rate)

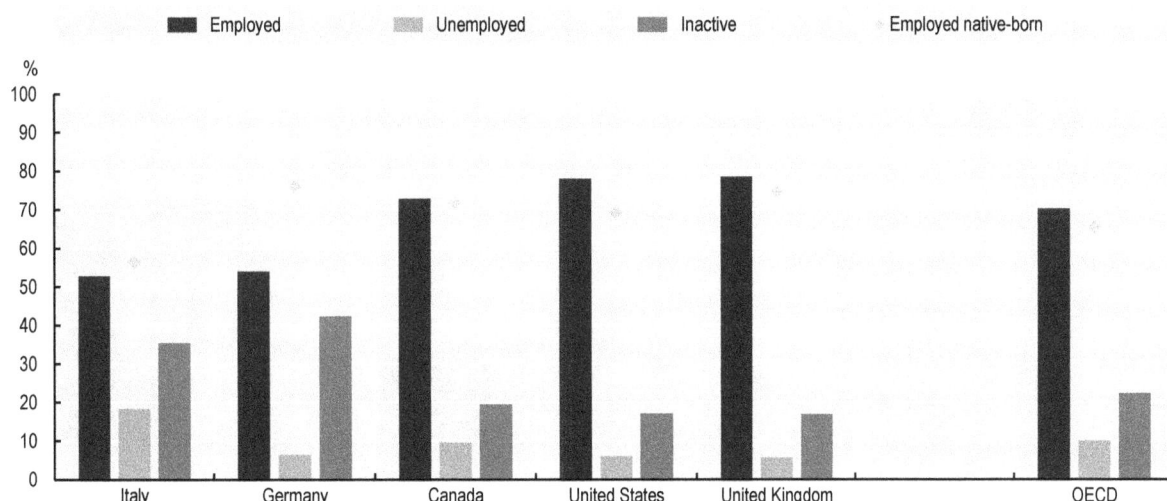

Source: OECD Database on Immigrants in OECD Countries (DIOC) 2015/16.

Figure 3.2. Employment rates of Ghanaian emigrants in main OECD destination countries, 2015/16

Share of working-age population

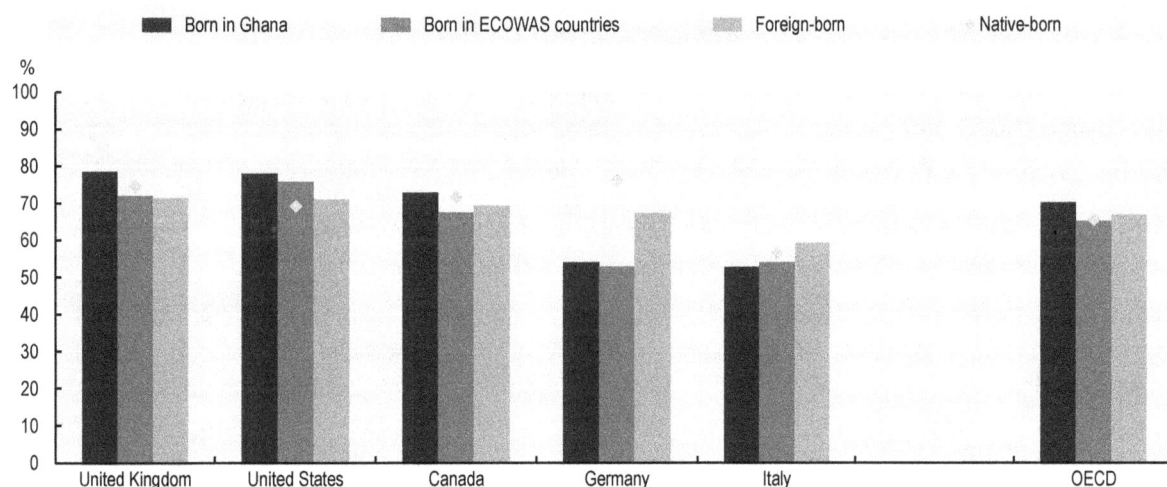

Source: Source: OECD Database on Immigrants in OECD Countries (DIOC) 2015/16.

Two leading destinations, where more recent data are available, provide evidence on other variables influencing labour market insertion. In terms of duration of stay, in the United States and Italy, employment rates of Ghanaian migrants increase the longer they have been settled in these countries (Figure 3.3). Among recent migrants – those who have arrived in the country within the past five years -, 32 and 63% were employed in Italy and the United States, respectively. Employment rates rise by 11 and 28 percentage points, respectively, among settled migrants (those residing in the country for over ten years). Relatedly, the acquisition of citizenship also appears as an important factor influencing access to the labour market. The employment rates of Ghanaian migrants with Italian citizenship are 9 percentage points higher than among non-naturalised migrants. In the United States, 84% of Ghanaian migrants with American citizenship are employed, versus 72% of those without American citizenship. The latter result holds even when controlling for the duration of stay.

Figure 3.3 Evolution of employment, inactivity and unemployment status among Ghanaian emigrants by duration of stay in Italy (2017/20) and the United States (2017/19)

Share of working-age population

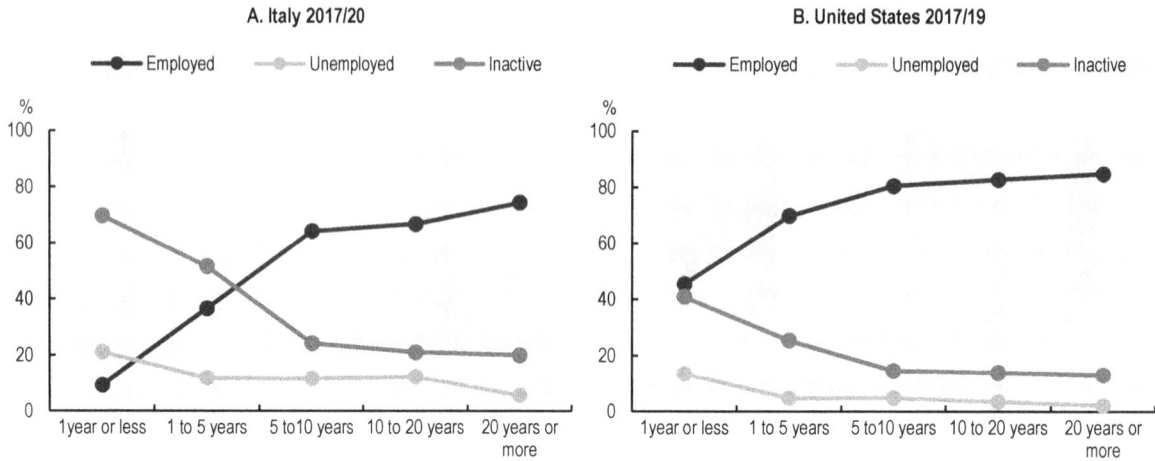

A. Italy 2017/20 — B. United States 2017/19

Legend: Employed, Unemployed, Inactive

Source: Italy: Istat Labour Force Survey, pooled data from 2017, 2018, 2019 and 2020; United States: American Community Survey 1-Year estimates; pooled data from 2017, 2018, 2019.

A relatively stable labour force participation with high heterogeneities

Between 2010/11 and 2015/16, the employment rates of Ghanaian migrants have remained relatively stable in the OECD area (Figure 3.4), with an increase of 1 percentage point during this period, a rate almost on par with the native-born population but weaker than the rate observed among ECOWAS migrants and the foreign-born population more generally. The evolution of employment rates, however, varies across destination countries, reflecting different stages of economic recovery in the aftermath of the 2008 global recession and the 2010 Eurozone debt crisis (Figure 3.5).

The picture is mixed in the English-speaking countries. In the United Kingdom and Canada, employment rates increased by 6 and 3 percentage points, reflecting a greater recovery than among the native-born populations. In the United States, the employment of Ghanaian migrants bounced almost at the same rate as the native-born population, although at a slightly lower rate than the foreign-born. Nonetheless, the average level of employment among the latter remained 7 percentage points lower than among Ghanaian migrants.

Figure 3.4. Evolution of employment rates in OECD countries, 2010/11 and 2015/16

Share of working-age population

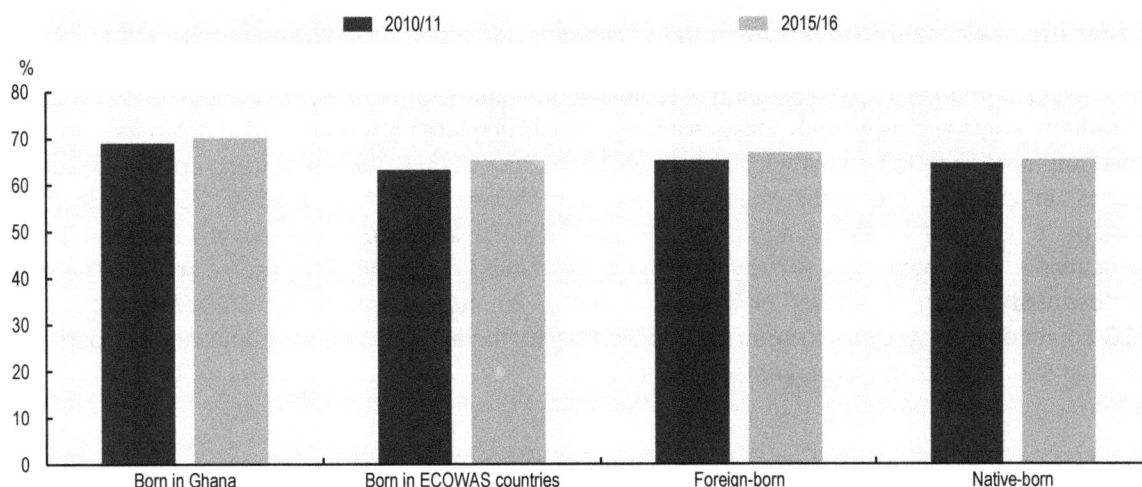

Source: OECD Database on Immigrants in OECD Countries (DIOC) 2015/16.

Figure 3.5. Evolution of employment rates among Ghanaian emigrants in main OECD countries of destination, 2010/11 and 2015/16

Share of working-age population

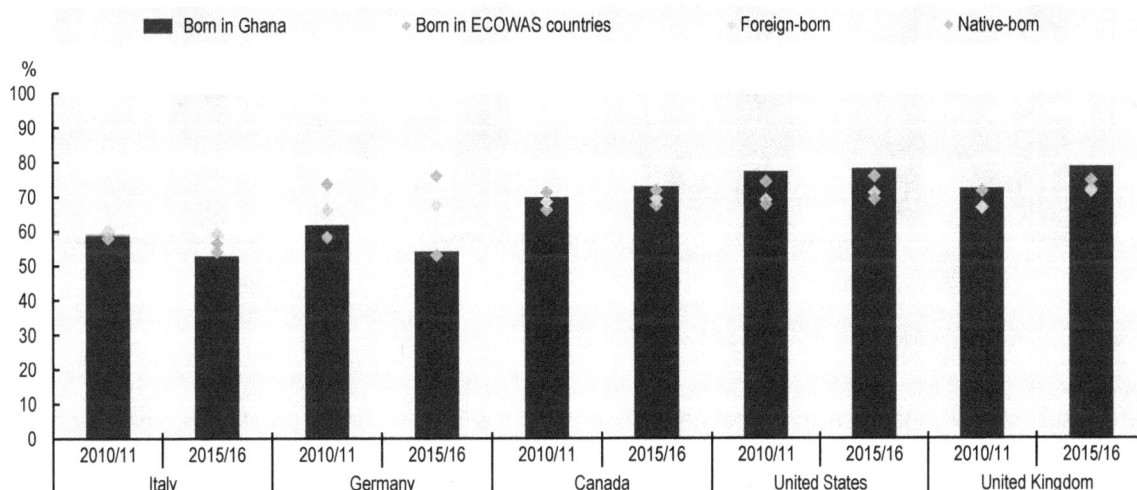

Source: OECD Database on Immigrants in OECD Countries (DIOC) 2010/11 and 2015/16.

Conversely, in other European countries, the trend is more negative. Ghanaian and ECOWAS migrants were similarly affected in Germany, and the employment gap with the native-born population increased during this period. While the employment rate for the native-born increased by 2 percentage points (1 percentage point for the foreign-born), ECOWAS and Ghanaian migrants' share in employment decreased by 5 and 8 percentage points, respectively. Further, unemployment rates also dropped in both countries (-10 percentage points in Germany and -4 percentage points in Italy), but inactivity rates rose sharply (+10 percentage points in Italy and +16 percentage points. in Germany). The dynamic is partially explained by the hardships faced by recent migrants in labour markets between 2010 and 2015

(OECD, 2016[3]). Emigrants already settled in these countries saw their situation unchanged, in general, but those recently settled faced more difficulties finding work opportunities in the aftermath of the economic crises.

Gender inequalities in the labour market remain salient for Ghanaian emigrants

While the labour market tends to be unfavourable to women, foreign-born women face a double challenge, both as immigrants and as women. Despite improvements in migrants' labour market outcomes, immigrant women are more likely to be unemployed than men (OECD, 2020[4]). The same trend applies to Ghanaian migrants: in 2015/16, the employment rate for women was 64% compared to 75% for their male counterparts, a gap of 11 percentage points (Figure 3.6). The absence of significant differences in terms of educational attainment rules out any human capital-related explanation for such disparity. The gender gap observed among Ghanaian emigrants is similar to that observed for ECOWAS emigrants in OECD countries. Nonetheless, the gap is narrower than for the average migrant population (17 percentage points.) or the native-born (15 percentage points.).

Figure 3.6. Employment rates of Ghanaian emigrants by sex, 2015/16

Share of working-age population

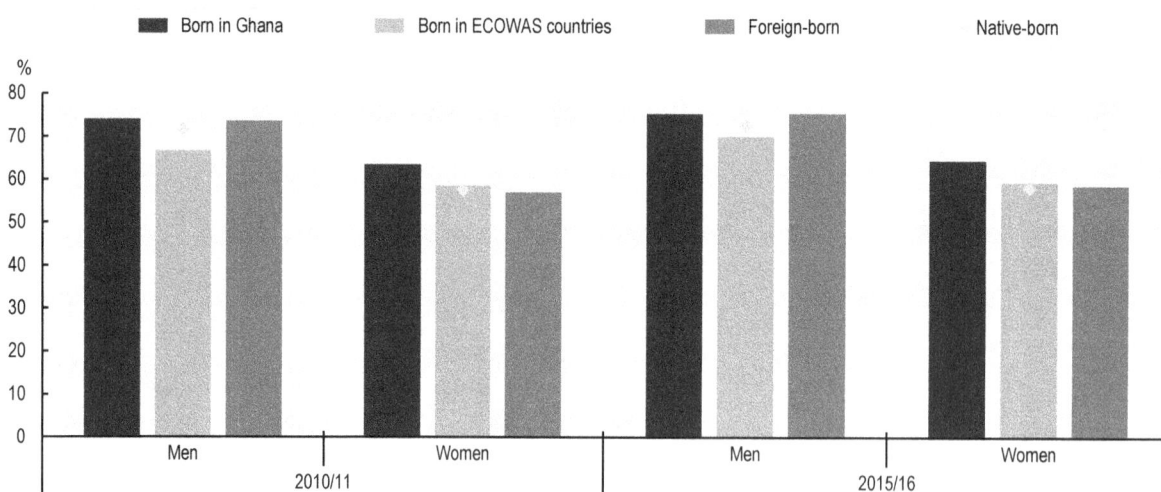

Source: OECD Database on Immigrants in OECD Countries (DIOC) 2015/16.

There is substantial variation across destination countries: the largest gender employment gap is observed in Italy, with a difference of 39 percentage points between men and women (Figure 3.7). Italy is a particular case in that the gender gap among the native-born is also the highest among the main destination countries, suggesting that, overall, women fare worse than their male counterparts in the labour market. Educational attainment does not account for this gap, as there are no significant differences between Ghanaian men and women. However, women are overrepresented among those who arrived in Italy within the past five years, confirming that men emigrate first and their families follow. Similar patterns of family reunification, reflected in lower employment rates among women, are also observed in the United States and Germany.

Conversely, in Canada and the United Kingdom, the gender employment gap is significantly lower and suggests that, within these corridors, women also emigrate as independent professionals. In the United Kingdom, the gender employment gap is 3 percentage points, the lowest among the main destinations and lower than among the native and foreign-born, as well as among ECOWAS migrants.

Figure 3.7. Employment rates among Ghanaian emigrants in main OECD destination countries by sex, 2015/16

Share of working-age population

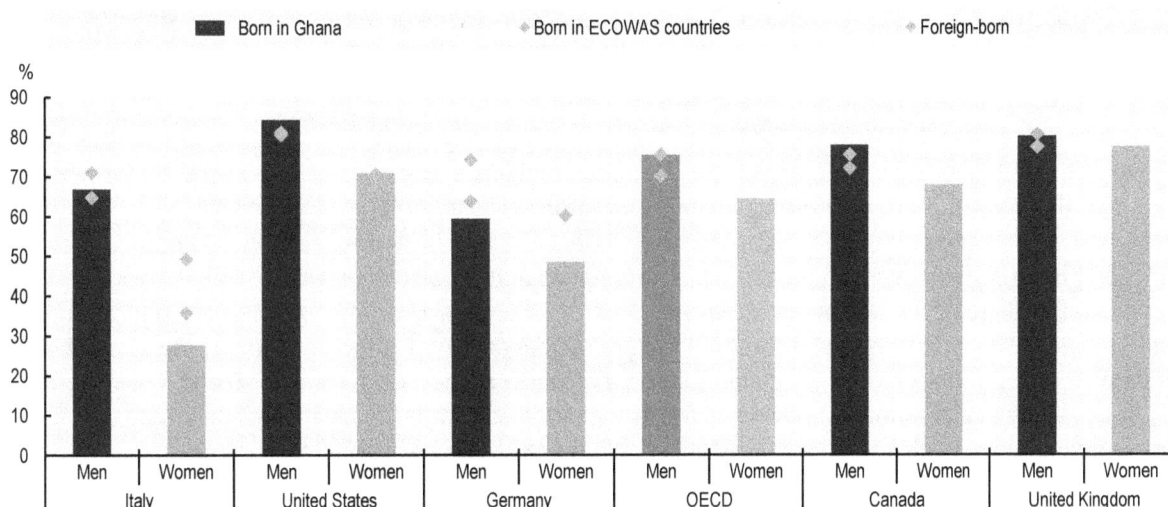

Source: OECD Database on Immigrants in OECD Countries (DIOC) 2015/16.

Highly educated Ghanaian emigrants have better access to employment

Regarding the relation between education and employment, Ghanaian emigrants with higher educational attainment fare better in the OECD labour market: in 2015/16, the employment rate among the tertiary educated was 82%. Such rate drops by 10 percentage points among those with medium educational attainment (upper secondary). It lowers by an additional 18 percentage points for those with low education (up to lower secondary).

Figure 3.8. Employment rates of Ghanaian emigrants by level of education, 2015/16

Share of working-age population

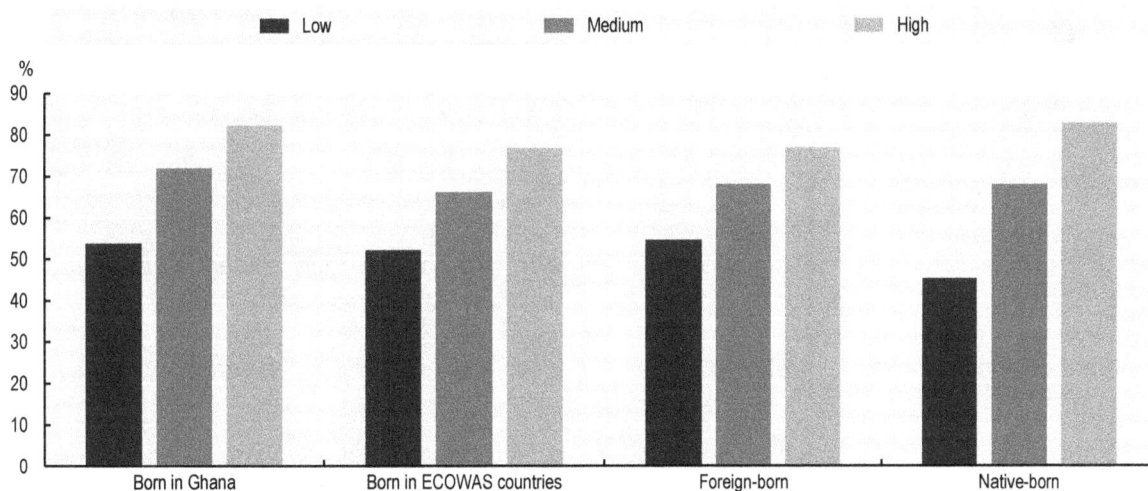

Source: OECD Database on Immigrants in OECD Countries (DIOC) 2015/16.

Employment rates among Ghanaian migrants in OECD countries were higher than among the average migrant and ECOWAS migrants at all educational levels suggesting higher employment returns to education for Ghana-born individuals. In fact, tertiary-educated migrants from Ghana fare almost as well as tertiary-educated native-born individuals.

However, despite their better insertion in the labour market, Ghanaian emigrants of working age remain more vulnerable than the native-born population. Indeed, Ghanaian migrants were more often unemployed at all levels of education than the native-born. At low and medium education levels, 15 and 11% of Ghanaian migrants, respectively, were unemployed compared to 12 and 8% of the native-born.

Further, the positive returns to education for Ghanaian emigrants are not observed across all destination countries (Figure 3.9). In Italy, the employment rate of those with tertiary education (5%) is substantially lower than those with low and medium education levels (51 and 65%, respectively). Although not in the same proportions, Ghanaian migrants with a tertiary education also fare worse than those with lower educational attainment in Germany. More than half of Ghanaian migrants with tertiary education were inactive in 2015/16. Nevertheless, a common feature of both countries is the very small proportion of highly educated individuals among the Ghanaian migrants of working age, accounting for 8 and 4% in Germany and Italy, respectively. Moreover, many of these highly educated migrants arrived only recently, further explaining their low employment rate. Results should therefore be interpreted with caution.

Figure 3.9. Employment rates of Ghanaian emigrants by level of education and destination country, 2015/16

Share of working-age population

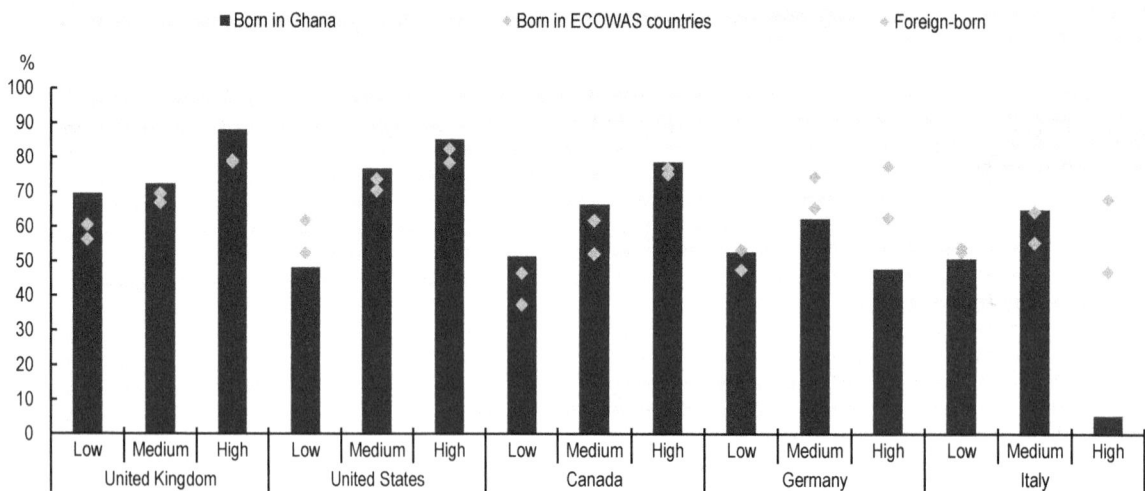

Source: OECD Database on Immigrants in OECD Countries (DIOC) 2015/16.

High employment returns to education among Ghanaian migrants are only evident in the three main English-speaking countries of destination. In the United States, just over half (54%) of low-educated Ghanaian migrants were employed in 2017/2019, compared to 77 and 85% of those with a medium and high level of education, respectively. At high levels of education, Ghanaian migrants are close to full employment, similarly to the native-born population.

The employment rate of Ghanaian emigrants with a high educational level was even higher in the United Kingdom: 88% were employed in 2015/16. This rate is 10 percentage points higher than for ECOWAS migrants and all foreign-born migrants. In Canada, the increase in employment rates from one level of education to the next was relatively linear: 52% for those with a low level of education, 67% for those with a medium level, and 79% for highly educated migrants.

Occupations and skills of Ghanaian emigrants

A substantial share of high-educated Ghanaian emigrants are overqualified

Despite the relatively high employment rates among tertiary-educated Ghanaian emigrants, there remains a significant mismatch between their qualifications and their occupations' skill levels. In 2015/16, almost half (43%) of tertiary-educated migrants from Ghana in OECD countries were overqualified in their occupation (Figure 3.10). If this rate was almost on par with the ECOWAS average (42%), it was significantly higher than for all foreign-born and native-born individuals (35 and 29%, respectively). Nonetheless, there are no significant differences between men and women, and these differences are less pronounced than among the native and foreign-born populations.

Box 3.1. Over-qualification: Definition and measure

Over-qualification occurs when an individual's level of formal education is higher than what the occupation held requires. It is estimated as the proportion of persons with a tertiary education degree who hold a low- or medium-skilled occupation. Education levels are measured using the International Standard Classification of Education (ISCED); high education level corresponds to ISCED Level 5 and higher. The level of qualification required for a position is measured using the International Standard Classification of Occupations (ISCO); high-skilled jobs belong to the first, second and third major groups.

Among immigrants, the over-qualification rate is an indicator of the degree of transferability of human capital across countries, as the qualifications and linguistic skills acquired in the country of origin are not always readily transferable in the host country, although it may also capture discrimination in the labour market, asymmetries of information on job availability, etc.

Across the main destination countries, there was no substantial variation in over-qualification rates. In the main English-speaking countries, where educational attainment is the highest, over-qualification rates did not exceed 45%. Among these three destinations, Canada was the only country where Ghanaian migrants were overqualified to a larger extent than other ECOWAS emigrants.

More recent data (2017/2019) from the United States confirms that over-qualification rates remain high, but affect women to a lesser extent than men: 38% of Ghana-born women were overqualified versus 43% of Ghana-born men. The recognition of a tertiary education diploma also plays an important role in accessing high-skilled positions. A third of Ghanaian emigrants who attended college or university in the United States – having arrived before the age of 18 or between 18 and 24 – are overqualified. Conversely, over-qualification rates affect 49% of those who arrived at an older age. The duration of stay also mitigates over-qualification: a third of settled emigrants from Ghana (having arrived in the United States more than ten years ago) are overqualified compared to 58% of recent emigrants from Ghana (having arrived in the United States less than five years ago). Relatedly, the acquisition of American citizenship improves access to high-skilled jobs: 38% of Ghana-born Americans are overqualified, a rate 15 percentage points lower than for Ghanaian emigrants without American citizenship (53%). These results are robust when controlling for duration of stay.

Figure 3.10. Over-qualification rates of Ghanaian emigrants by sex and destination country, 2015/16

Share of tertiary-educated workers

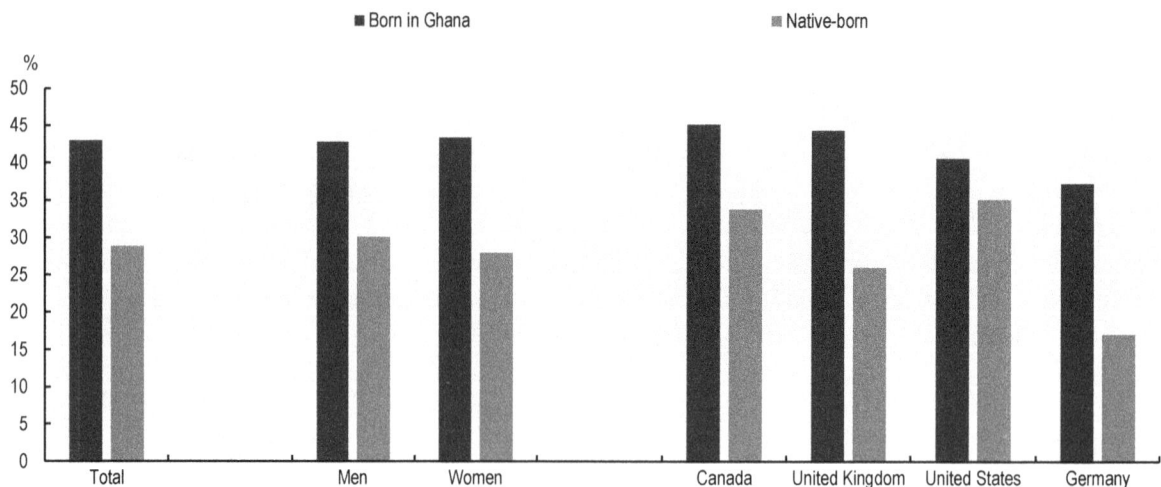

Note: Italy is not included because of the very small population of Ghanaian emigrants with a high level of education.
Source: OECD Database on Immigrants in OECD Countries (DIOC) 2015/16.

Ghanaian emigrants are highly overrepresented in low-skilled occupations

Over-qualification rates among Ghanaian emigrants reflect in their occupational distribution at OECD countries of destination, as they tend to be overrepresented in low-skilled occupations. A third (34%) of Ghanaian emigrants of working age held an elementary occupation in 2015/16, compared to less than one-tenth of the native-born (Figure 3.11). The share of Ghanaian emigrants in elementary occupations is twice the share among the foreign-born (17%).

In OECD countries, excluding the United Kingdom and the United States, Ghanaian emigrants are mainly occupied in craft and related trades occupations (17%), services and sales occupations (14%), and as plant and machine operators (11%). If both men and women are mainly employed in elementary occupations, Ghanaian women are overrepresented in services and sales (20% versus 10%). Men are overrepresented in craft and related trades occupations (23% versus 7%) and as machine operators (15% versus 4%).

One in ten Ghanaian emigrants were engaged as professionals (9%) and 2% as managers, compared to 17% and 5% among the native-born. Overall, 19% of Ghanaian emigrants occupy high-skilled positions, either as managers, professionals or technicians and associate professionals.

Figure 3.11. Occupational distribution of Ghanaian emigrants by sex in OECD countries, 2015/16

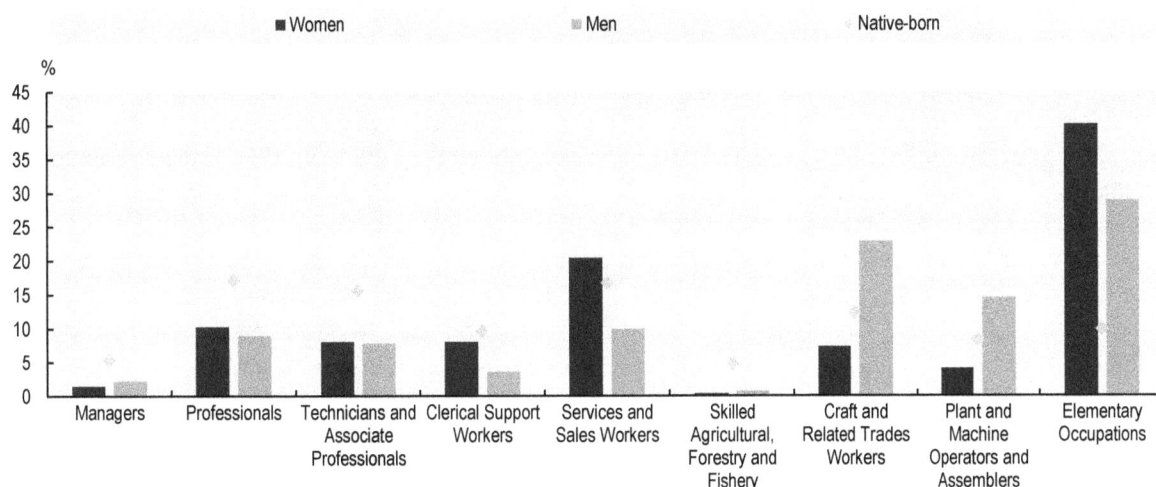

Note: Excludes data from the United States and the United Kingdom. Armed forces occupations are not listed in the chart as they are not a main source of employment for Ghanaian emigrants.
Source: OECD Database on Immigrants in OECD Countries (DIOC) 2015/16.

Ghanaian emigrants' main occupations differ according to their destination country

The occupational distribution of Ghanaian emigrants varies by destination country (Figure 3.12). In Italy and Germany, the majority are employed in elementary occupations (40 and 47%, respectively), compared to 7% in Canada. In the latter country, almost half (43%) of Ghanaian emigrants are employed in high-skilled occupations, either as professionals, technicians or managers. Particular needs in the Canadian labour market and related migration policies explain these results. Canada welcomes the highest number of high-skilled workers thanks to an elaborate immigration system (OECD, 2019[5])

Figure 3.12. Occupational distribution of Ghanaian emigrants in three main destination countries, 2015/16

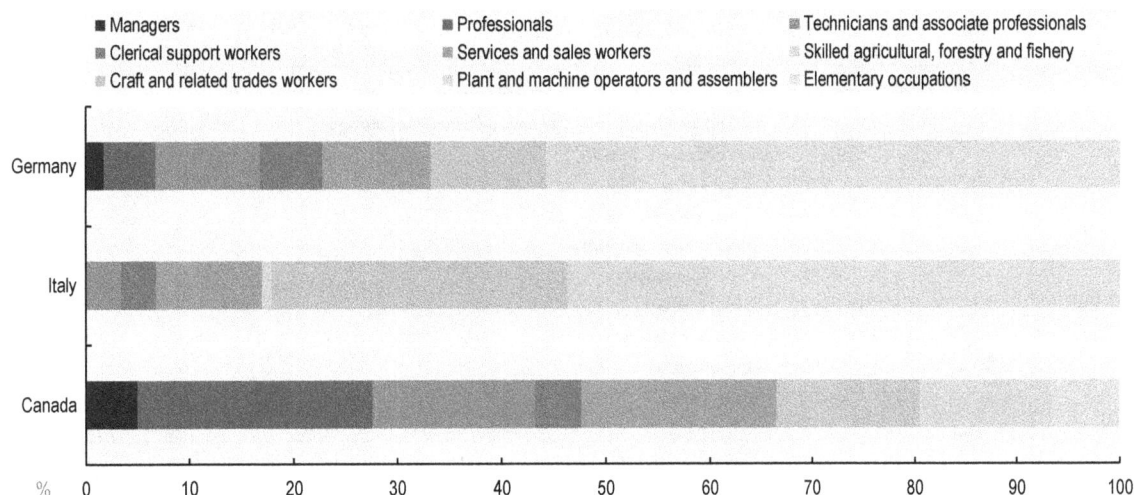

Note: Armed forces occupations are not listed in the chart as they are not a main source of employment for Ghanaian emigrants.
Source: OECD Database on Immigrants in OECD Countries (DIOC) 2015/16.

In English-speaking countries, Ghanaian emigrants are overrepresented in health professions

An overrepresentation in health-related occupations compared to the native-born characterises the occupational distribution of Ghanaian emigrants in English-speaking countries. This phenomenon has been documented in the literature as it represents an important challenge for national health care provision (Anarfi, Quartey and Agyei, 2010[6]; IMO MHD RO Brussels, 2011[7]; IOM, 2020[8]). Emigration intentions of health professionals from Ghana are very high (49% of nurses in 2013/2014) due to a combination of factors, which include low wages, difficult working conditions, low social status (Pillinger, 2011[9]) as well as exposition to violence (Boafo, 2016[10]). Ghana ranks among the top 20 origin countries of nurses working in the OECD area. While very few nurses in OECD countries were trained in Ghana (3%), more than a third (35%) of Ghana-born nurses, corresponding to 18 350 nurses, were working in OECD countries in 2015/16. Regarding doctors, 17% of those trained in Ghana and 30% of those born in Ghana worked in OECD countries in 2015/16 (Socha-Dietrich and Dumont, 2021[11]).

In Canada, 11% of Ghanaian migrants in employment held a health-related position in 2015/16, of which 59% were health professionals. These shares were similar for ECOWAS emigrants but 3 and 4 percentage points higher than for all native- and foreign-born workers, respectively. In the United Kingdom, about 5 800 Ghanaian migrants of working age were employed as health professionals, corresponding to 9% of all Ghanaian workers in the country. In addition to health professionals, a substantial share of working-age migrants from Ghana in the United Kingdom held a personal-care occupation (15%), including nurses.

In the United States, more than a quarter of the Ghana-born working population held a health care-related occupation in 2017/2019: 14% were employed as health care practitioners or held another technical occupation and 15% were employed in a health care support occupation (Figure 3.13). Ghanaian migrants hold such positions at higher rates than the native-born (9%, corresponding to -20 percentage points). Further, female Ghanaian migrants hold health-related occupations at higher rates than their male counterparts (46% versus 16%). In contrast, Ghana-born men are mostly represented in transportation-related occupations (15%), followed by office and administrative support occupations (11%).

Figure 3.13. Occupational distribution of Ghanaian emigrants in the United States, 2017/19

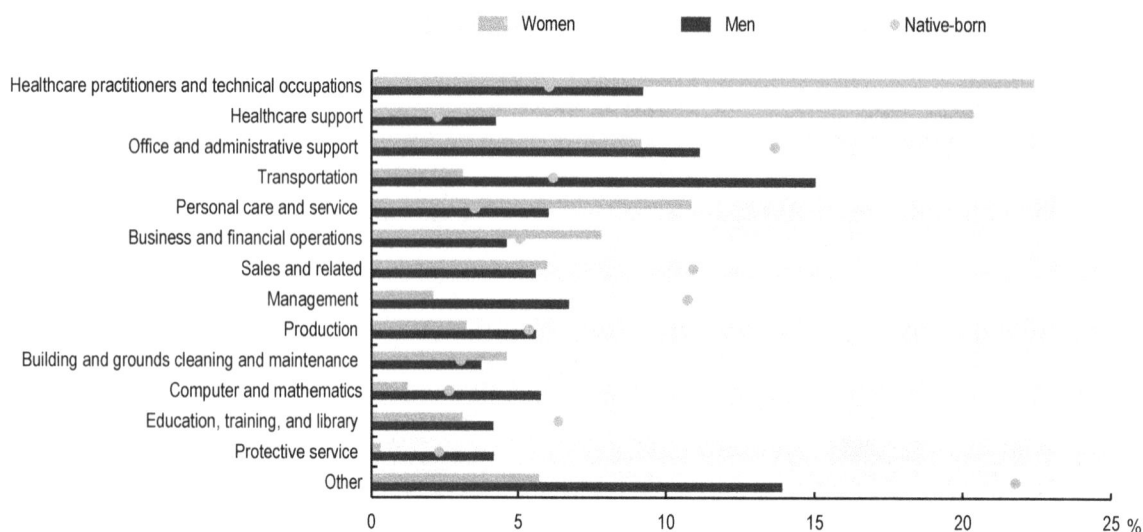

Note: Other occupations include: Farming, Legal, Arts, Military, Physical and Social Sciences, Construction, Architecture, Maintenance, Social Service, Food preparation.
Source: American Community Survey (ACS) pooled data for 2017, 2018 and 2019.

Figure 3.14. Occupational distribution of Ghanaian emigrants in the United Kingdom, 2015/16

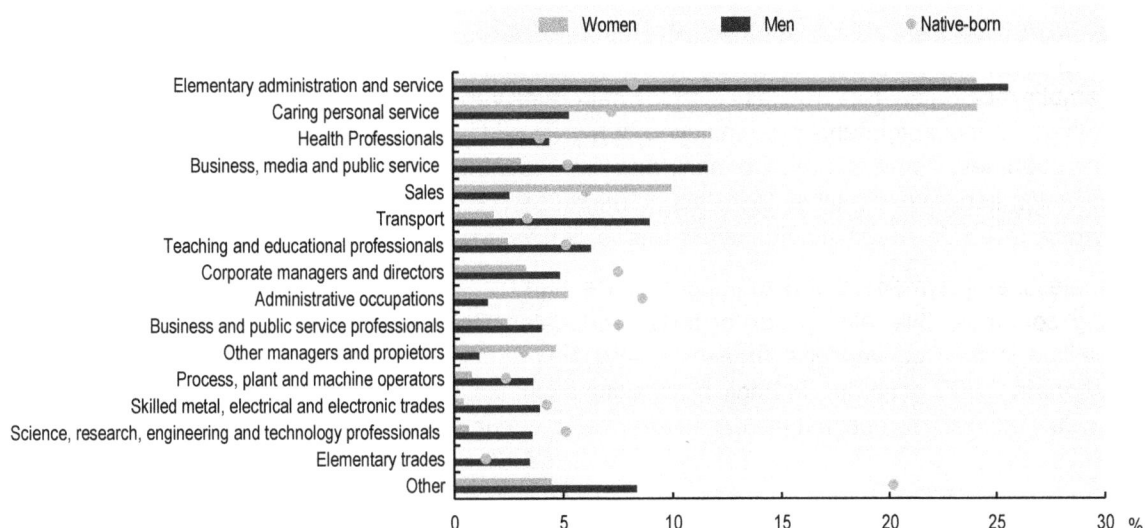

Note: Other occupations include: leisure and travel, skilled construction, secretarial occupations, protective service, customer service.
Source: OECD Database on Immigrants in OECD Countries (DIOC) 2015/16.

In Benin and Togo, Ghanaian emigrants are mainly employed in agricultural and service occupations

In two African countries for which there are data available, the occupational distribution of Ghanaian migrants reflects a high concentration in agricultural and services occupations. Half of the Ghanaian migrants in Benin and Togo were occupied as skilled agricultural and fishery workers at the last censuses. Services and related trades occupations also employ significant shares of Ghanaian male migrants. In Benin and Togo, two-thirds and a half of women, respectively, were employed as service workers. The agricultural sector also employs a significant share of Ghana-born women (38%).

Figure 3.15. Occupational distribution of Ghanaian emigrants in Benin and Togo, 2013 and 2010

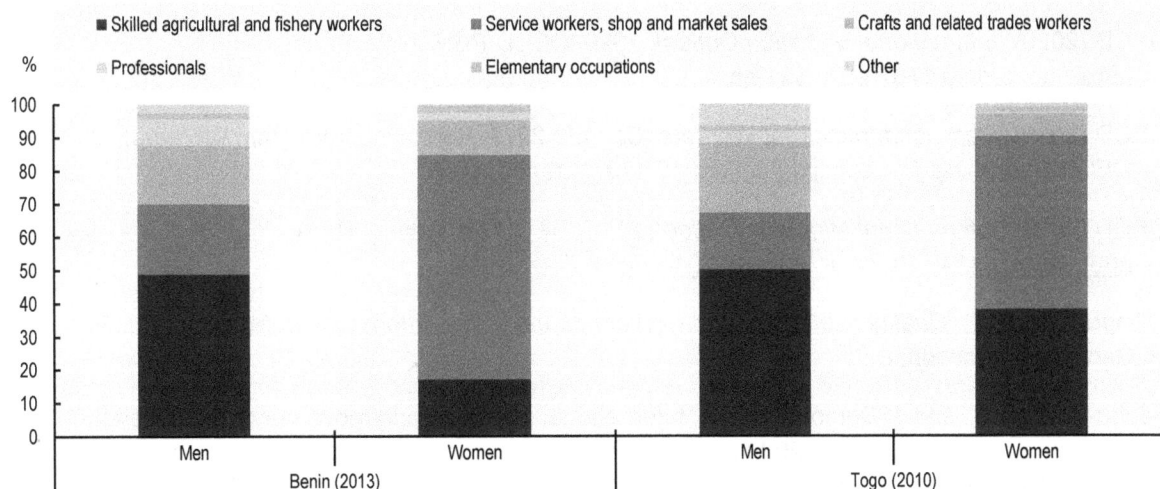

Note: Most recent census data available at the time of publication.
Source: Benin 2013 Census via IPUMS; Togo 2010 Census via IPUMS.

Conclusion

The labour market insertion of Ghanaian migrants in OECD countries is relatively positive. More than three-quarters of those aged between 15 and 64 years old participate in the labour market and evidence low unemployment rates. Nevertheless, employment rates vary substantially from one destination country to the other. Ghanaian migrants are employed at higher rates than the native-born population in English-speaking countries. Conversely, in Germany and Italy, countries of more recent immigration, where other types of migration patterns other than labour migration predominate, Ghanaian migrants present low employment levels. Insertion into the labour market is even more difficult for women born in Ghana.

Nevertheless, employment returns to education are high for Ghanaian emigrants, particularly in English-speaking countries. Still, almost half of tertiary-educated Ghanaian emigrants in the OECD area are overqualified in their occupations. Indeed, a substantial share of Ghanaian workers holds elementary occupations in OECD countries. In English-speaking countries, however, Ghanaian emigrants, and women in particular, are overrepresented in health care related occupations.

References

Anarfi, J., P. Quartey and J. Agyei (2010), *Key determinants of migration among health professionals in Ghana*. [6]

Boafo, I. (2016), "Ghanaian nurses' emigration intentions: The role of workplace violence", *International Journal of Africa Nursing Sciences*, Vol. 5, pp. 29-35, https://doi.org/10.1016/j.ijans.2016.11.001. [10]

IMO MHD RO Brussels (2011), *National Profile of Migration of Health Professionals – Ghana*, International Migration Organisation Regional Office Brussels. [7]

IOM (2020), *Migration in Ghana: A Country Profile 2019*, International Organization for Migration. [8]

Marabello, S. and B. Riccio (2018), "West African Migrations to Italy: Anthropological Analysis of Ghanaian and Senegalese Politics of Mobility in Emilia Romagna", *Revue européenne des migrations internationales*, Vol. 34/1, pp. 127-149, https://doi.org/10.4000/remi. [2]

Morath, V. (2015), *The Ghanaian diaspora in Germany*. [1]

OECD (2020), *International Migration Outlook 2020*, OECD Publishing, Paris, https://doi.org/10.1787/ec98f531-en. [4]

OECD (2019), *Recruiting Immigrant Workers: Canada 2019*, Recruiting Immigrant Workers, OECD Publishing, Paris, https://doi.org/10.1787/4abab00d-en. [5]

OECD (2016), *International Migration Outlook 2016*, OECD Publishing, Paris, https://doi.org/10.1787/migr_outlook-2016-en. [3]

Pillinger, J. (2011), *Quality healthcare and workers on the move: International migration*, Public Services International. [9]

Socha-Dietrich, K. and J. Dumont (2021), "International migration and movement of doctors to and within OECD countries - 2000 to 2018: Developments in countries of destination and impact on countries of origin", *OECD Health Working Papers*, No. 126, OECD Publishing, Paris, https://doi.org/10.1787/7ca8643e-en. [11]

Annex A. Data sources of Ghanaian emigrants

OECD Database on Immigrants in OECD Countries (DIOC), 2000/01, 2005/06, 2010/11 and 2015/16

The Database on Immigrants in OECD Countries (DIOC) covers the OECD destination countries for which data were collected both in 2000/01, 2005/06, 2010/11 and 2015/16. The main sources of DIOC data are national administrative registers and population censuses. In the censuses carried out in 2000/01, almost all OECD countries collected information on the country of origin of emigrants, so that it became possible to have an comprehensive overview of the numbers of migrants in OECD countries (for more general information on DIOC, see d'Aiglepierre et al. (2020[1]). Where censuses were not available or incomplete, labour force surveys were used as a substitute.

DIOC contains information on populations from more than 200 countries of origin residing in OECD destination countries. The main variables are country of residence, country of birth, gender and level of education. Other variables – age, duration of stay, labour force status and occupation – can be cross-tabulated with the core variables but not always with each other. Data on employment and occupation are available for the population aged 15 years or older. In Chapter 3 of the review, the focus is on individuals of working age, that is those between 15 and 64 years. Two variables contain information on citizenship.

OECD International Migration Database (2000-19)

The *OECD International Migration Database* covers annual flows of legal migration. The annual flows of foreign population inflows and outflows by nationality are estimated on the basis of national population registers, residence and/or work permits, and specific national surveys. This database is largely based on the individual contributions of national correspondents (the OECD Expert Group on Migration) and covers most OECD countries as well as the Baltic countries, Bulgaria and Romania. The data has not necessarily been harmonised internationally and should therefore be interpreted with caution. For example, flows to the United States only include permanent migrants, while other countries also include temporary migrants such as seasonal workers, students or refugees. In addition, the registration criteria and the conditions for obtaining a residence permit vary across countries, which has important repercussions on the measurements obtained. Finally, irregular migration is only partially covered, so it is important to note that actual migration flows are likely to be higher than legal migration flows.

Eurostat database on residence permits issued to third-country nationals (2008-20)

Data on residence permits concern third-country nationals (persons who are not citizens of the European Union) receiving a residence permit or authorisation to reside in one of the European Union member states, the EFTA countries (Iceland, Lichtenstein, Norway and Switzerland) or the United Kingdom. Data are based on administrative sources, with the exception of the United Kingdom, and are provided mainly by home departments or immigration agencies. As the United Kingdom does not have a residence permit system, the data for this country relate rather to the number of citizens from outside the European Union who arrive in the territory and are authorised to enter the country under certain immigration categories. A residence permit corresponds to any authorisation valid for at least 3 months issued by the authorities of a member State allowing a third-country national to legally reside on its territory.

Gallup World Poll Data

The Gallup World Poll covers a large range of behavioural and economic topics and provides information on self-reported emigration intentions of the Ghanaian population. This survey is conducted in approximately 140 countries based on a common questionnaire, translated into the predominant language of each country. Each year since 2006, more than 100 questions have been asked to a representative sample of around 1 000 persons aged 15 and above. In some countries, Gallup collects oversamples in cities or regions of special interest. The survey collected a total of more than 16 000 observations from Ghana (about 1 000 per year from 2006 to 2021).

Afrobarometer Survey (2016/2018)

The Afrobarometer survey has been conducted every two years since 1999 in a growing number of African countries to measure people's attitudes on governance, democracy, the economy, civil society, public services, justice and pan-Africanism. The 2016/18 survey wave is the seventh and final survey wave available. Conducted in 34 countries, it includes questions on emigration intentions of individuals living on the African continent, such as perceived difficulties in crossing borders, migration status, intentions to emigrate, most likely country of emigration, and main reason for emigrating. The nationally representative samples comprise between 1 200 and 2 400 individuals aged 18 or older. The answers to these questions can be cross-referenced with several socio-demographic characteristics such as age, gender, education level and labour market status. Given the sample sizes, the results based on this survey should be apprehended with caution.

International Students (UOE Database)

The UNESCO-OECD-Eurostat (UOE) data collection on education statistics is compiled from national administrative sources, as reported by ministries of education or national statistical offices. To capture student mobility, a distinction is made between resident foreign students – i.e. foreign students who are resident because of their parents' prior migration or their own – and non-resident foreign students, who came to the country expressly to pursue their education. International students are defined as students with permanent residence outside the reporting country, and data on non-citizen students are used only where information on non-resident foreign students is unavailable. Data on international students are only available from 2013 onwards.

Reference

d'Aiglepierre, R. et al. (2020), "A global profile of emigrants to OECD countries: Younger and more skilled migrants from more diverse countries", *OECD Social, Employment and Migration Working Papers*, No. 239, OECD Publishing, Paris, https://doi.org/10.1787/0cb305d3-en.   [1]